Misunderstandings

False Beliefs in Communication

Georg Weizsäcker

OpenBook
Publishers

ii

ISBN Paperback: 978-1-80064-881-4
ISBN Hardback: 978-1-78374-051-2
ISBN Digital (PDF): 978-1-80511-138-2
DOI: 10.11647/OBP.0367

Cover: Thomas Gainsborough, Conversation in a Park (1746), Louvre Museum,
https://commons.wikimedia.org/wiki/File:Thomas_Gainsborough_-_Conversation_
in_a_Park_(1746).jpg
Cover design: Jeevanjot Kaur Nagpal

The publication of this work was supported by the Open Access Publication Fund of Humboldt-Universität zu Berlin, funded by the Deutsche Forschungsgemeinschaft (DFG, German Research Foundation) – 491192747. The publication of this work was further supported by the CRC/Transregio 'Rationality and Competition: The Economic Performance of Individuals and Firms' (TRR 190), funded by the Deutsche Forschungsgemeinschaft (DFG, German Research Foundation) – 280092119.

DFG Deutsche
Forschungsgemeinschaft
German Research Foundation

Georg Weizsäcker is a behavioral economist. He obtained his PhD in Business Economics at Harvard University, has taught at the London School of Economics and Political Science and at University College London, and is now Professor of Economics at Humboldt-Universität zu Berlin. His research lies in the areas of experimental economics, decision theory and applied microeconomics, with numerous contributions on the understanding and interpretations of other people's statements and choices. He is a Fellow of the European Economic Association, was appointed to numerous scientific committees and boards, and currently serves as the spokesperson of a research center on applied behavioral economics funded by the German Research Foundation.

Contents

1 Introduction: Should we talk?   1

2 Having a conversation   9

3 Seeing what we don't see   17

4 Talking   31

5 Listening   47

6 Seeing what they don't see   61

7 Perceiving how they talk   73

8 Perceiving how they listen   89

9 In higher order: Seeing their view of our view   101

10 Conclusion   107

11 Bibliography and further reading   109

Index   121

Author's acknowledgements   127

Chapter 1

Introduction: Should we talk?

Three tales that feature in this book

The governor exudes power. Rachel watches him from across the conference table. His occasional laughter is loud, his knowing smile invites others to speak, but not for too long. Today is his first visit to the institute. The institute's director has introduced the senior researchers sitting around the table, Rachel among them, and two of her colleagues have already made their contributions to the conversation. "Who else?" says the governor.

Dimitri finds Agniezka at the elevator. They are on their way back to their offices, returning from an inter-group competition where they jointly presented a product – and suffered a defeat against a group of colleagues who showed a more effective design. Dimitri and Agniezka had worked on their idea for about a year, with high hopes to win today and move to the next stages of development. Now, they have to reconsider. The elevator door opens.

Steve carries his ball in a swift walk around the block. He is looking for other kids to play with. Turning a corner, he almost bumps into Ralph. Ralph is much older, at least nine, and he is one of the schoolyard bullies. Today, on the sidewalk, he does not look bully-ish at all. His shoulders are drooping, his facial expression is sad and he leans against the wall of a building, as if seeking its support. The street is empty and Steve can see that Ralph was alone before he, Steve, had turned the corner.

     https://doi.org/10.11647/OBP.0367.01

About the book

Should we talk? This book treats this question, and many others, as being empirical in nature: if we were to live through a given situation in 1000 parallel lives, where in one half we talked and in the other half we didn't talk, in which of the halves would we fare better?

The results of such a thought experiment vary between Rachel, Dimitri, and Steve – or any other conversation that we may experience. Costs and benefits depend on the details of the conversation. Every conversation is different and rich in detail. Why, then, is this book so thin? The main reason is that the book, while asking questions with the usual scholarly care, is quite brief in its way of answering these questions. More precisely, it contains one empirical answer per question – `appearing in separate font` – and this answer is valid only for a specific context. The reader is invited to extrapolate, asking the same question for other conversations of interest.

Such extrapolation is, luckily, easy. Having conversations is an ubiquitous experience. Countless literatures give examples of noteworthy conversations, in the social sciences, business studies, psychology, and many other fields.

While the answers in this book are few, the set of questions is suprisingly exhaustive. The book's 18 questions about human conversations are, in a specific sense, *all* relevant questions up to a well-defined point. They systematically cover the ways in which a conversation can go wrong.

So, what are these ways of going wrong? This book describes a particular set: inaccurate expectations. We may fail to judge the situation correctly. We may think that things are plausible when they are not, in a way that reduces our utility. We may misjudge our partner in conversation, or the situation, or the language. The book thus approaches conversations through the expectations that they come with. It formulates 18 *misunderstandings*: ways in which expectations are off target. Misunderstandings may be the ugly ducklings within the family of beliefs. But hey, here they are. Sometimes, they may even be more important than their not-so-ugly cousins. It is therefore worthwhile to study their nature.

This leads to asking about the reader's benefit – why read this book? The main benefit is, perhaps, to learn something new in behavioral economics. Communication is a fast-growing research area in economics, and especially in microeconomics and organizational economics. Experimental measurements of communication abound, too. But misunderstandings, despite appearing very frequently, are an uncharted area of research. Little is known about them, at least in the scholarly literatures of economics and business studies.

To help fill this gap, the book aims to give an overview of misunderstandings. It discusses the events, statements and actions that the misunderstandings are about – the "targets" of beliefs that are relevant in a conversation. In parallel, the book discusses the methods to measure the beliefs and it reports evidence on the distance between the beliefs and their targets. All of this follows an empirical approach. Each of the 18 questions put forward here is an empirical question, i.e., in principle its answer can be found through a well-designed measurement.

A notable distinction between this book and the descriptions of most other non-standard beliefs in behavioral economics is that misunderstandings are not described here with reference to a theoretical benchmark. Instead, a misunderstanding is just a belief that misses its target, empirically speaking. The book uses its conceptual parts merely as a springboard.

The non-theoretical exposition also means that the reader does not have to go through elaborate economic models. Having a general understanding of statistics suffices to follow the analysis. As a note of caution, however, the reader should know that parts of the analysis, especially in the book's second half, are game-theoretic in nature, and thus non-trivial.

Credit where credit is due: psychology scholars have a long and valuable tradition of documenting misunderstandings and, more generally, all kinds of non-optimal beliefs and behaviors. The book includes some of these findings in its discussion. Interdisciplinarity is, always, key in behavioral economics.

The second benefit for the reader also has an interdisciplinary flavor: he or she will learn about the logic of human language. The book ventures outside of both psychology and economics: to discuss false beliefs in communication, one needs to ask basic questions about the interpretation of messages. Such questions are the object of study in the field of pragmatics, a highly developed part of linguistics and the philosophy of language. This field, too, has a tradition of studying misunderstandings, and significant parts of the book's analysis rely on insights from it.

The author hastens to add that the book is not a suitable introduction to any part of psychology or pragmatics. It merely makes observations about these fields and adapts some of their basic ideas from the vantage point of an economist. The main observation about pragmatics is a simple one: many of its ideas can be suitably studied via a description of beliefs. Economists are used to studying beliefs – but the beliefs that pragmatists emphasize are largely new to economics.

A well-known economic anecdote may serve as illustration. In July 2012, in the midst of the euro crisis, the European Central Bank's president Mario Draghi made history with a short utterance: "Within our mandate, the ECB will do whatever it takes to save the euro. And believe me, it will be enough." The statement was an instant hit – media reported it widely and the statement is now believed to have caused a market turn-around: speculation against the government finances of multiple countries, and against the euro, subsided. Markets returned to normal.

How can a simple statement be so influential? Or, expressed in terms of beliefs: What did the listeners expect when they heard it? What did Draghi expect when he said it?

A large part of the answer is linguistic. The statement carries much meaning and strength by alluding to several important contexts at once. First, Draghi points out that the scope of ECB's activities is wide ("whatever it takes"). This was understood to indicate that the ECB would buy government bonds at a large scale if necessary. Second, he points to the depth of the bank's pockets ("it will be enough"). Third, he points to the fact that he is a credible source of information about the previous two contexts and that the market traders, and all other listeners, know less about them ("believe me").

The third of these contexts is especially relevant: presidents of central banks have an almost hard-wired commitment to being credible. Draghi ties this credibility to his knowledge about what the ECB can do. This is the context that he wants the listener to think about. A context where he, Draghi, is the master in the ring, which gives the statement its strength: the listener has no alternative but to believe him.

A feature of his statement, one that it shares with other successful statements, is that the listeners understand these relevant contexts although Draghi only ever-so-slightly alludes to them. But how? In a complicated world with a vast set of candidate contexts, how do the listeners learn what the talker refers to? It is a little miracle when it works.

A second example, also from the policy world, describes a misunderstanding. In April 2021, Germany's political parties were in an open race for the succession of Angela Merkel as chancellor. Much of the political debate focused on Covid, at a time when the roll-out of vaccinations was still slow and a new wave of infections swept across Germany. Armin Laschet, a party leader and a front-running candidate for the chancellorship, made a public statement on Covid regulations. It was widely followed by the media, not least because Laschet himself had built up suspense by pre-announcing the statement a few days earlier. Then he finally made it: "We need a bridge lockdown." The idea being, as he explained, that another temporary restriction of public life, while costly, may serve as a bridge to better times: the lockdown would give time to create more vaccine-induced immunity in the population. However, Laschet failed to gain support for his initiative. Instead, large parts of the public criticized him for inventing the new expression "bridge lockdown". It was argued that using the positive-sounding word "bridge" to counter-act the public's negative emotions about the restrictive measures amounted to being borderline deceitful. Also, commentators noted that all Covid lockdowns have the nature of serving as bridges to better times, such that Laschet said little that was new. (He later also lost the election.)

Laschet suffered from a basic misperception: he believed that the new, better-sounding wording (with an unusual sound also in the original German, "Brücken-Lockdown") would make the public more favorable to his position. Alas, it did not. The choice of words drew attention away from the statement's substance – which was not generally viewed as unreasonable – to the more superficial topic of the intention of the politician who uttered it. The statement lost its meaning by revealing that Laschet wanted it to sound meaningful. With such a strong emphasis, the public wanted more content than Laschet offered.

The later chapters of the book will discuss how such linguistic mechanisms may, or may not, work in general. As a one-sentence preview of this discussion, they may work because the listeners can see the conversation through the eyes of the talker. They interpret what the talker intends to achieve with the statement and what context the talker refers to. They search for the relevance of intentions and contexts, guided by the statement to find a useful insight (in Draghi's case) or not (in Laschet's case).

The reader may already recognize the sound of game theory here: a listener who thinks strategically does not only solve his or her own problem, but solves the talker's problem, too. Such second-order thinking is quite a task in a conversation because the listener needs to do several things at once: anticipate the preferences of the talker and consider the context that the talker refers to, among the many possible contexts that exist. It is complicated, and an invitation for misunderstandings, but not impossible.

Related questions may spring to the reader's mind, too. Doesn't the talker do the same, and solve the listener's problem? If so, don't both people need to engage in another layer of iterated strategic thinking, where each thinks how the other person, conversely, thinks about them? And so on – how many layers are there?

The book discusses conversations, by and large, with only two layers of strategic thinking. It sets out the definitions of the first-order beliefs that are relevant for the talker and the listener, then discusses these beliefs at length, then turns to the other person's expectations about them (i.e., second-order beliefs). As Chapters 9 and 10 will argue, the analysis could go further and consider beliefs of third and higher order, but they also argue that such a higher-order analysis would perhaps be less valuable than the analysis of lower-order thinking. Beliefs of higher order become less and less easily measurable, and studying them is often not necessary: many key insights arise without reference to higher-order thinking.

Chapter 11 gives some leads to further readings. The chapter also explains where each of the substantial ideas used in this book originate from. (This is important because the book's main body contains no bibliographic references. The chapter serves to give appropriate credit to other authors and literature, in the same way that other books or articles have bibliographic endnotes.)

Readers of all backgrounds will find that the book is short and dense. It is best to read it slowly. Or, perhaps, to complement its reading with that of other texts. The book is, however, a stand-alone, self-sufficient piece.

A note to course instructors who consider teaching with the aid of this book: it's best if you judge for yourself whether it works for your course. The author has repeatedly test-taught the book as the main reading for a Master's-level student seminar on the behavioral economics of communication. Students of different backgrounds can deal with the interdiciplinary material in very different ways, going deeper into secondary readings according to their own interests. The expositional style of asking questions aims to teach students about empirical research in a simple and transparent way. Finally, note that many different ways of splitting up the material are possible, making the book suitable reading for a half-term course or a full-term course.

The book's structure follows a rigorous but unconventional logic. The next chapter lays the groundwork and describes the book's assumptions about conversations. Essentially, it describes an analytical framework based on subjective expected utility theory (which implies large degrees of freedom). The subsequent six chapters formulate and discuss the 18 misunderstandings, three per chapter. Each is presented as a question about a possible misunderstanding, digging deeper as the book progresses. Chapters 3, 4, and 5 cover possible failures of first-order beliefs, and Chapters 6, 7, and 8 cover analogous failures of second-order beliefs. Chapters 9, 10, and 11 discuss how one may find more possible misunderstandings and how else the 18 questions can be placed in the wider literature on human communication. These three chapters are not part of the book's main body (reading them is very much optional) but they hopefully add clarity. The book's focus on misunderstandings is, definitely, not an excuse for avoidable confusion.

As the reader may have guessed already: the examples involving Rachel, Dimitri and Steve, which will re-appear throughout the book, are fictional and only serve for illustration. The `evidence from scholary research`, in contrast, is real. It is only a thin layer of evidence but appears to show a pattern: many beliefs in communication are not very sophisticated in that they do not react to one or several pieces of information to a sufficient degree. Either the talker or the listener fails to take something into account.

Future measurements will tell us about this pattern's robustness. As described above, the book is written at a relatively early point in the sequence of the relevant research that it describes. It is much more about questions than about answers.

Chapter 2

Having a conversation

Three conversations

Agniezka and Dimitri stand in silence as the elevator moves up one floor, and another one. Dimitri then addresses the issue of the lost competition: "This was bloody. Not the end of the story, though. We will hit back."

Agniezka turns her head and gives Dimitri an expressionless stare. She says, "Hopeless. Make it your bloodbath, not mine. I'm done with this project, sorry." The door opens and Agniezka leaves the elevator.

Rachel straightens her back. "Mr. Governor, please consider the urgency of research on stolen artifacts. We ask you to look into the possibility of funding a new center of competence that studies the provenance of cultural property. How did this property leave its home? The Cambodian statues in western museums and collections are a good example. Many of them were looted in postwar turmoil. This was publicized in newspapers and we verified the reports with scientific studies. But for contexts outside of Cambodia, the facts about provenance are mostly unresearched. We need more structured knowledge, we have enormous work before us and we need your help with it."

The governor hears her out and replies, "Rachel, another great line of research! We are on the same page and I much admire your spirit and that of your colleagues. I well recall how you and I first met, in a panel discussion on cultural policies, planning a common agenda. Let's continue this process! You also know that we already do a lot for top-level research in our museums, through our funding programs." He pauses briefly. "We will continue these efforts, too – but here and now, we have to move on." He looks at the

9

 https://doi.org/10.11647/OBP.0367.02

researcher sitting next to Rachel.

For a few seconds Steve looks at Ralph, the older boy, who turns around and looks back at Steve. His shoulders are not drooping any more.

"Wanna play?", says Steve, holding the ball in his hands.

Ralph's face assumes its usual, hostile look. He walks straight towards Steve and slowly, almost routinely, pushes him with his overweight arms, then walks away.

Simplifying restrictions

A conversation has multi-faceted content, much more than meets the eye. The three conversations of Rachel, Dimitri and Steve are similar only at the surface – the talker wants the listener to do something, the listener rejects it – but they strongly differ in terms of their contexts, their human characters, their languages, their outcomes, and in the future events that they induce.

The analysis starts by narrowing things down. It focuses on what is uncertain. When people talk and listen, they do this with incomplete knowledge. Three aspects of uncertainty arise: about *actions, issues, and types*.

Actions are everything that people do during or after the conversation. This includes all their possible statements: statements are actions.

To notate the action (or statement) of person i, the book uses the symbol a^i and it is understood that the action is one out of a given set A^i of possible actions for person i, i.e., $a^i \in A^i$.

The book will keep this and other mathematical notations to a minimum and it sometimes even describes variants of the basic set-up without notating them formally. For example, a person's action may sometimes depend on another person's action without a mathematical notation for it.

Issues are things that are exogenous to the actions. They are things that cannot be changed. The book refers to them as the "state of the world" (or simply "state"), which is notated by ω and is, generally speaking, unknown at the time of the conversation. The true state is an element of a larger set of possible states, $\omega \in \Omega$.

Not all is unknown of course, as everyone knows *something* about the state of the world. The information that person i has about ω is notated by the symbol I^i_ω. It is convenient to describe I^i_ω as a subset of Ω that contains ω; this indicates that person i, if she pays attention to her information, can deduce that some states are ruled out: those that lie in Ω but not in I^i_ω. She does not know the exact value of ω but she can safely conclude (later, we will say, it is "manifest" to her) that ω lies in I^i_ω.

Most likely, the people in the conversation each know something different. The conversation may help to exchange their views.

Types, notated by θ^i for person i, describe the person's preferences. They are person-specific and include everything that is idiosyncratic: desires and tastes, capabilities and necessities.

Note that a person's preference for certain outcomes can be related to her behavioral constraints. If person i strongly dislikes an outcome, this is similar to the case where her action set A^i does not contain an action that leads to this outcome. The book's analysis keeps these things apart, for simplicity: θ^i describes person i's preferences for a fixed set A^i, i.e., it describes which of the available possible outcomes (and actions) she likes relatively better than others.

In its general discussion, appearing in normal font and black color, the book does not specify the exact nature of actions, issues and types. In any given conversation, they may be either explicit and in the open, or hidden in the background. For a successful analysis of a given situation, one should specify these aspects in sufficient detail but also simplify where appropriate, focusing on the main features of the situation.

At the surface, Steve's simple question ("Wanna play?") asks about Ralph's preference regarding a ball game. Ralph's possible reactions, however, are not all playful: he may turn to violent bullying, especially now that Steve saw him in a state of despair. The analysis may therefore collect Steve's possible statements into two groups: those that address Ralph's state of despair, e.g. by asking about it, versus those that address more normal things. We also separate the set of Ralph's possible reactions in two groups, describing whether he is violent or not, and likewise, his set of possible types:

his despair may either fuel his tendency to be violent, or it may reduce it. Steve's own type, in contrast, plays no important role in this conversation. The relevant issues, or states of the world, are the unknown events that underlie Ralph's despair. A further relevant unknown are Steve's future actions: will he tell other kids about what he saw, or not?

Rachel focuses her statement on a set of future actions that she hopes to provoke – the governor's possible support for a new research center. She could talk about many different things but here, too, we may simplify by restricting her choice to be between two topics: the process on cultural policy taht has already begun (and that the governor refers to in his response) or the new topic of provenance. We may also describe the governor's possible reactions as binary: either supporting Rachel's research with new funds, or not supporting it. We note that the relevant state of the world comprises not only the substantive topic of conversation but also the professional context, i.e., the unusual situation of the governor's visit as well as the presence of other colleagues. We also note that the personalities, or types, of Rachel and the governor are in the background; no-one addresses them openly – only the personal tone of the governor's response alludes to them.

Dimitri is hoping to keep Agniezka on his team and to jointly prepare an aggressive push in the development of their project. The circumstances of the conversation are fairly complex but for our discussion we again focus on a small set of issues: the team's chance of success if the team stays together, the team's chance of success if the team splits up, and Dimitri's and Agniezka's history of past actions. This history is in the background but influences the conversation, and more elaboration on it will follow in later chapters. We can also restrict attention to two types of statements that Dimitri may make in the elevator: statements about the possible scenario where Agniezka remains on the team – he indeed chooses to make such a statement – versus statements about the possible scenario where the team splits up. In either case, his statement is bound to be fairly bad-tempered, owing to his disappointment about the lost competition. Agniezka's reaction, in turn, can be simplified to either staying on the team, or not. (Notice also that Dimitri does not have to say anything during the elevator ride. We observe that this may be the wiser course of action, but the subsequent discussions will take it as given that Dimitri is the talker.) The relevant types are Dimitri's and Agniezka's preferences vis-á-vis these possible statements and vis-á-vis the future actions that may arise in each of the possible scenarios.

The book makes additional restrictions, to narrow things down further.

The first restriction is to consider only single steps of a conversation: there are two people in the conversation – the two interlocutors – where one person says something and the other person reacts.

One may try to apply the book's analysis to longer conversations with more than one step. To do so, one could simply view everything that is said in the conversation as a single statement. The analogy is vague, however, and it is therefore best to focus on single-step conversations.

Future actions of the interlocutors may, of course, have a foreshadowing effect on the present conversation. For example, the possibility of telling other children about the encounter with Ralph is on Steve's mind. The book does not analyze how the interlocutors choose such future action – they are not part of the present situation. It merely considers that future actions are plausibly influenced by what is said now. For a streamlined notation, all future actions are subsumed as parts of the interlocutors' action sets, even though the interlocutors cannot pick them in the present conversation.

As a second restriction, the book assumes that each person knows their own type. Introspection is assumed as faultless. In contrast, the other person is somewhat mysterious. In formal notation, let $I_{\theta^j}^i$ be person i's information about person j's type, and let Θ^j be the set of possible types for j. Then, the above assumption is that $I_{\theta^i}^i = \theta^i$ and $I_{\theta^j}^i \subset \Theta^j$.

The third restriction is that the uncertainty about other people's types is assumed to be statistically independent of the uncertainty about the state of the world. This means that one cannot learn anything about the state from learning about the type, and vice versa. It is another simplification; in its absence the exposition would be cumbersome, with little insight added.

Translating this assumption into a formality is not possible yet, as we have not introduced any formalities about probabilities and beliefs. Once they are introduced, further down in this chapter and the subsequent ones, making the assumption of statistical independence is straightforward. The book's analysis also assumes that the interlocutors agree to this simplification.

More simplification comes from the fourth restriction: person i's realized utility from the conversation depends *only* on the realized values of the uncertain aspects. These are: the actions of the two interlocutors (a^i, a^j) (including their statements in the conversation and everything they do afterwards), the realized value of the state of the world ω, and the person's type θ^i.

The fifth restriction is perhaps the most controversial: everyone deals with the uncertainty in a subjectively "rational", expectation-based way. That is, while the people in the conversation cannot know the uncertain aspects when having the conversation, they form subjective expectations about them and react to these expectations.

Formally, the fourth and fifth restrictions amount to assuming that person i's utility from the conversation is given by

$$u^i : A^i \times A^j \times \Omega \times \Theta^i \to \mathbb{R}$$

(which means that u^i is a function with arguments a^i, a^j, ω, and θ^i) and that the chosen action a^i maximizes i's subjective expected utility, i.e., she acts to maximize the expected value of u^i given her subjective expectations.

The book's focus is on these subjective expectations. For brevity, call them *beliefs*. The book simply asks, "What are the beliefs that would justify leading the conversation in the way that people lead it?"

The reader may wonder, why ask such an indirect question about underlying beliefs? Why not ask questions about the conversation itself?

The answer is twofold. First, the book can rely on the existing literatures on decision theory and game theory. These are impressive bodies of literature that describe, among other things, the existence and other properties of beliefs that justify actions. Without going into detail, it is safe to say that the book solidly stands on the shoulders of giants.

Second, a key observation lies at the heart of the book: conversations cannot be correct or false in an unambiguous way, but beliefs can be correct or false. Moreover, one can measure whether they are correct or false.

The next chapters therefore ask whether the beliefs about the uncertain aspects are distorted. For formal notation, the book uses the symbol P^i_x for person i's subjective belief about unknown item x. It is a probability distribution over x's possible values and will depend on information that person i has. For example, i's belief about the state of the world after seeing her information set I^i_ω is $P^i_\omega(\cdot|I^i_\omega)$, a probability distribution over the elements in Ω. As another example, $P^i_{a^j}(\cdot|I^i_{\theta^j})$ is i's belief about j's action a^j, after learning information $I_{\theta j}^{i}$ about j's type, and it is a probability distribution over the elements of A^{j}.

This leads to the final simplifying restriction: common knowledge of the conversation's basic ingredients. The sets of possible actions, types, and states of the world, are assumed to be commonly known by the interlocutors and the information structure that governs who may receive what information is also assumed to be commonly known by them. That is, while each interlocutor does not know what the other knows, they do agree on what this knowledge could conceivably be. Moreover, the fact that each interlocutor reacts to their belief, as specified by subjective expected utility, is also taken as commonly known. The interlocutors do not know each other's beliefs, but know the fact that the other interlocutor reacts to *some* beliefs.

Yet, we note well that beliefs are not identical to information: information is taken as given, but beliefs may be off target. To continue using the notation above, I_{ω}^{i} is given but $P_{\omega}^{i}(\cdot|I_{\omega}^{i})$ is not. Person i will, of course, lead the conversation in a way that depends on $P_{\omega}^{i}(\cdot|I_{\omega}^{i})$. We are therefore interested in measuring it.

Taken together, the above simplifications allow a precise description of the scope of possible belief distortions. This is the book's main subject, whose discussion begins after the next short section.

A quick final comment on notation: to avoid all-too-frequent use of "person i" and "person j", the text henceforth also refers to "us" and "them", where possible.

Talking and listening

When we talk, the conversation moves *their* beliefs. We can thus influence their actions in a way that improves our utility. When we listen, the conversation moves *our* beliefs: about the issue and about their (the other person's) type. Knowledge about these aspects also informs us about their subsequent actions. Upon listening, we can thus use our improved knowledge to choose a better action ourselves.

Steve's question steers Ralph's attention away from the events underlying his despair (the most relevant issue) to the everyday topic of the ball game.

He also keeps Ralph from thinking about the consequences that arise from the fact that Steve saw him in his present situation. It is noteworthy that Steve does not give Ralph any information but he nevertheless affects his beliefs. The strategy avoids the dangerous terrain, and Ralph sees no reason to change the topic, either. Steve's statement was successful.

Rachel does not have much success with her statement and we may speculate that one reason for it is that the statement is rather impersonal. She does not, in particular, give the governor any motive to follow her funding suggestion. His belief about the political consequences arising from questions about the provenance of art did not change anywhere near as much as would be necessary to choose the action that Rachel hopes to induce.

Not to ignore: there is also a direct utility effect that arises from both our talking and our listening. Talking has value over and above the exchange of information, and so does listening.

Dimitri may feel better after saying what he says, but his statement fails to have the desired effect on Agniezka's belief: that she may benefit from staying on Dimitri's team. If anything, it has the opposite effect.

Prior to saying something, the direct utility effect from doing so is evident to us: we know what we can say and how much we like saying it (the book's analysis assumes it, anyway – recall that these are simplifications). We also know our type. All other described effects are unknown. We cannot know what they would say if we let them talk. We cannot know how they would react to any statement that we may make. We cannot know the state of the world.

On the basis of our beliefs about these unknowns, we decide how we talk. We also understand that their situation is similar: we know that they, too, form beliefs and react to them. We even know that they know that we form beliefs and react to them. This is indeed a very rational way of conversing.

But rational does not mean optimal. It only means that a conversation follows systematic patterns, which makes it worthwhile to study it. Optimality requires far more: that beliefs are accurate. This is what the 18 questions are all about.

Chapter 3

Seeing what we don't see

This chapter asks the first three empirical questions about beliefs. They address what we expect ex ante, before the conversation begins.

Since we do not care about their type *per se* (within the limits of the conversation), the relevant uncertainty is about two unknown aspects: their actions and the state of the world. Question 1 and Question 3 address the former and Question 2 addresses the latter.

In what way are the questions in this chapter about ex-ante beliefs, as opposed to ex-post beliefs? There are two answers to this. First, at the beginning of the conversation, it may not be clear whether they or we will listen or talk, respectively. Chapter 4 will discuss the beliefs for the case that they listen and we talk, and Chapter 5 for the case that they talk and we listen. Here, in Chapter 3, this is still open.

Second, Chapters 4 and 5 will proceed by conditioning the analysis on the possible statements: what happens if we say X, and what if we say Y? Here, in Chapter 3, we do not yet consider how beliefs are conditional on statements. In this sense, the beliefs discussed in Chapter 3 are prior beliefs, and those discussed in Chapters 4 and 5 are posterior beliefs. Yet, as we now discuss, even prior beliefs are conditional.

Question 1: Do we underappreciate that every person is different?

We have to gauge our partner in conversation. We have to judge their situation and predict their actions. Every person is different and, hence, every

17

   https://doi.org/10.11647/OBP.0367.03

person's actions are different. If we think that we already know how they will act, then we might regard the conversation as unnecessary.

One possible goal of the conversation is that we want to find out about their information. Do we know what they might tell us?

Another reason for wanting to know their actions is that our utility depends on the combination of their actions and our actions. Accordingly, what we believe our best actions to be depends on what we believe their actions to be.

Their actions, in turn, depend on their type. We have some information about their type. Do we use it well? This question thus asks how our belief about their actions *conditions on our information about their type.* Does this conditioning move our belief far enough?

Researchers who work on belief elicitation often distinguish two properties of beliefs: discrimination and calibration. Applied to our context, discrimination is the extent to which we differentiate at all between different people, in the sense that we expect different actions from them. Calibration measures the extent to which these conditional beliefs are correct.

'Do we underappreciate that every person is different?' is, by and large, a question about discrimination. The subsequent 17 questions in this book are also of this type. They all ask whether our conditional beliefs show a particular deviation from their target: we may differentiate too little.

Stating the question more formally, from person i's perspective:

$$\text{Is } P_{a^j}^i(\cdot|I_{\theta^j}^i) \text{ too close to } P_{a^j}^i(\cdot)?$$

Rachel's belief about the governor's way of leading the conversation is ignorant of his type. She has met the governor before and she is aware of his political record, but she fails to draw any inference from the information that she has about his type.

The governor, in turn, was briefed about the people around the table and anticipates that Rachel may use the opportunity to push a new research agenda, instead of continuing the previously-started inititative. Also, he is always prepared to receive requests for funds (and is unlikely to engage with them).

The book repeatedly uses the wording "too close to" to describe the empirical possibility that two subjective probability distributions – here, $P^i_{a^j}(\cdot|I^i_{\theta^j})$ and $P^i_{a^j}(\cdot)$ – are closer to each other than the actual distributions of their targets, i.e., the random variables that they refer to. Given what person i knows about θ^j, she may conceivably predict person j's action better than she actually does. Her conditional belief would be more accurate if she anticipated better that certain types choose certain actions and if she combined this insight with her information $I^i_{\theta^j}$, which indicates something about the type that she faces.

The conditional belief can err in many other ways, too. Beliefs are probability distributions – assigning a probability to each possible value of an unknown variable – and their distortions may tend into many different directions. The expression "too close to" alludes to a particular one: person i does not differentiate person j's types as much as the true data generating process.

We also notice the vagueness of the expression: a precise formal expression for "too close to" would require a proper distance measure between distributions. This can be defined with some effort, but is skipped here as it would not substantially aid the discussion. The reader will have a good idea what "too close to" means, even without a formal definition.

Taking this good idea for granted, one can notice a further property of the formulation: it asks about a directed hypothesis. The question can be answered with a simple "yes" or "no" – and the answer indicates a particular bias. It is also noteworthy that the question does not attempt to clarify why the answer is what it is. The question is purely empirical.

Later chapters of the book will provide candidate explanations of why the answer is what it is. For now, the focus lies on the methods for answering Question 1. How does one measure this?

The easiest case is that the to-be-predicted action, a^j, has only two possible values that the placeholder · in person i's belief can take on; call them A and B. The belief assigns a probability to A and a probability to B. The two probabilites sum to one and the belief is therefore fully described by a single number, the subjective probability of A. (As the reader noticed, our simplified discussions of Rachel, Dimitri and Steve view the actions as binary, wherever possible.)

In this case, a suitable measurement of person i's conditional belief requires *(i)* observing the information $I^i_{\theta j}$ that person i has about person j and *(ii)* eliciting the belief about the probability of the event that $a^j = A$ from person i.

Measuring these things is straightforward. A key advantage of a laboratory study is that the experimenter can control the information that person i has about person j, $I^i_{\theta j}$, or at least important parts of it. A second key is that the experimenter can ask whatever she wants. She can, for example, ask person i:

"Is person j more likely to choose A than B?"

The answer indicates whether or not $P^i_{a^j}(A|I^i_{\theta j})$ lies above 50 percent. Voilà, a bound on the conditional belief.

Or, the experimenter can ask for numeric values:

"Expressed in percentage probabilities, how likely is it that person j chooses A?"

Or, if the experimenter expects that the participants are not sufficiently experienced with probabilities, he or she can also refer to frequencies:

"Out of 100 repetitions of this experiment, in how many cases would person j choose A?"

Another possible method is that the experimenter may use a graphical tool to let the participants allocate probability mass. Which of these methods is best depends on the situation and on the eloquence of the instructions. Each of the methods has been shown to work.

But what is the *unconditional* probability $P^i_{a^j}(\cdot)$?

This is harder to measure because one usually observes person i with only one value of information, $I^i_{\theta j}$. One does not observe what person i would predict with any other value of her information, or without her information.

One possible solution is to consider another group of participants in the role of person i who receive no information about person j. The belief of these participants may be taken as a $P^i_{a^j}(\cdot)$.

As a second possible solution, the experiment can match each participant in the role of person i with a different partner in the role of person j. For each pair, person i receives some information about person j and the experimenter asks person i what they expect person j to choose. This elicits the conditional belief $P^i_{a^j}(\cdot|I^i_{\theta^j})$ for different information sets $I^i_{\theta^j}$ and the experimenter can calculate the population-wide unconditional belief $P^i_{a^j}(\cdot)$ as the aggregation of these conditional beliefs, averaging over the values of $I^i_{\theta^j}$.

Both solutions work in principle. There is, however, a fundamental way in which the second approach is preferable: it takes the fact that *some* information is given as given. Conditionality – here and throughout the book – should be understood as the belief being conditional on the *value* of the information and not on the fact that information is available.

So far, so good – but still not there. The experimenter also needs to measure the "actual distributions" that the beliefs are all about. What is person j likely to do?

Towards this measurement, the experimenter uses the second group of participants, acting as person j. The experimenter measures two proportions in this group: the proportion of A-choosing participants among all participants in the group (this is the actual frequency that the unconditional belief $P^i_{a^j}(A)$ tries to predict) and the proportion of A-choosing participants among those participants for whom a given information $I^i_{\theta^j}$ applies (...that the conditional belief $P^i_{a^j}(A|I^i_{\theta^j})$ tries to predict).

The difference between these proportions can be compared to the analogous difference in beliefs, yielding the answer to Question 1.

A famous economic decision-making experiment is the ''Trust Game''. In its basic version, one player decides whether to END the game immediately or to SEND some funds to the other player. To simulate the productivity of an economic interaction, the experimenter multiplies the sent amount by a factor greater than 1. The second player therefore either receives nothing (if the first player chooses to END) or receives more than the amount that was sent (...SEND). The game's main point of interest is that the second player can now PAY some funds back to the first player, or RUN and keep it all. Depending on the first player's belief about the

second player's PAY/RUN choice, it may therefore be optimal for
the first player to END or to SEND. Binzel and Fehr (2013) play
this game in a poor neighborhood of Cairo, Egypt, and each participant faces two pairings: they play either with a friend or with
a stranger. In each case, the participants acting as the first
player know whether their partner is a friend, with whom they
arrived together at the experiment, or a person who is randomly
chosen from the other participants. The frequency of PAY is statistically larger for friends than for strangers (72% versus 55%)
but the beliefs of the participants in the role of the first player
are not: when playing with a friend or a stranger, respectively,
40% and 49% of these participants say that they expect their partner to choose PAY. That is, they tend to trust friends less, not
more, than strangers. (This belief difference is statistically
insigificant.) We also see a general tendency to be pessimistic:
calibration is imperfect in the sense that the unconditional, average belief in PAY is too low. This book's focus, however, lies
on the degree of discrimination. In the present game, participants do not realize the sizable increase in PAY frequencies when
playing with friends rather than strangers.

Question 2: Do we underutilize our knowledge of the world?

The second uncertain aspect is the state of the world. Knowing it is important because we can choose actions that adapt to this knowledge.

But how much can we know? The state of the world is high dimensional.
What are the dimensions on which we need more information? What are
dimensions that influence our utility? What are dimensions on which the
conversation can inform us? And conversely, what are dimensions that help
us predict the conversation?

This asks about what dimensions we *should* focus on. What we *do* focus
on is another matter. In many cases, it is a matter of accessibility. Some
parts of the state of the world are easy to think about. We have words for
them, or lively memories. Other parts are more elusive. Are the dimensions
that are accessible to us also the ones that are relevant for us?

This leads to the distinction between things that are known to us and things that we *could* know if we were to focus on them. Let us say that these things are *manifest* to us.

In a rich world, a lot of things are manifest to us when we enter the conversation. Most of these things are unknown to us, in the sense that our actions and statements do not reflect them, but nevertheless they are manifest: we could be made aware of them and our actions and statements could reflect them. This is important in a conversation, not least because some of these manifest things may be pointed out by our partner in the conversation.

The distinction between known things and manifest things resonates with the book's differentiation between information and beliefs. A person's information describes the totality of things that are manifest to her. For person i, it is given by the sets I^i_ω and $I^i_{\theta j}$. In the book's remaining parts, the full information that includes all of these manifest things will often be called the *circumstance* of person i. It is a rather sophisticated description – everything that person i could know.

In contrast, the beliefs of person i, denoted by P^i_ω and $P^i_{\theta j}$, are likely to be less sophisticated: they describe what she actually considers in her choices and statements. They differentiate only along the dimensions that person i pays attention to.

(In an important way, beliefs go further than information: they specify probabilities for the uncertain states of the world. But beliefs may nevertheless be rather unsophisticated.)

We thus re-phrase our question: instead of asking whether the manifest things are the right ones, we ask whether our beliefs differentiate between the right dimensions. Would our utility increase if our beliefs differentiated more along other dimensions?

Having accurate beliefs is not just about differentiating but it is also about getting the quantities right (recall: discrimination and calibration). It requires that we find the right measure of weighing different dimensions against each other. How important is a given piece of additional information, relative to what we believe without considering this piece of information?

It is convenient to state this question, too, through conditional beliefs. Incorporating a new piece of information means forming a conditional probability, where the conditionality refers to the new piece of information.

$$\text{Is } P^i_\omega(\cdot|I^i_\omega) \text{ too close to } P^i_\omega(\cdot)?$$

Dimitri does not yet have a clear view about how the disappointing events of today's competition affect Agniezka's and his collaboration. He jumps to a tentative conclusion, vaguely describing a course of action that he believes to be available to them: "We will hit back." Given how little he knows, it may have been better to not conclude anything, and/or to ask Agniezka for information.

Agniezka enters the conversation with a more pessimistic view about the collaboration with Dimitri, and with more knowledge about the issue. In secret, she already hedged her bets during the last few months, by establishing contact with the competitor team, about the possibility of joining them. Before entering the elevator, she realized that today's competition has greatly reduced the options for her team with Dimitri.

To give an empirical answer to this question, the experimenter needs to measure, or control, the information I^i_ω. Experiments are well suited to do this because the controlled design can govern the information flow.

In its extreme form, an experiment can introduce a stylized set-up where the entire information structure is fully under control. The experimenter describes prior probabilities of ω's possible values, and explains how additional information is generated. For example, that it comes from random draws from one of several urns that have known proportions of balls of different colors. The state ω is the unknown identity of the urn from which a ball is drawn, and the information I^i_ω is the color of the drawn ball. Upon observing the ball's color, the participant can update about ω.

In such a stylized set-up, the unconditional belief $P^i_\omega(\cdot)$ comes for free: the experimenter may take it for granted that the participants agree to the prior probabilites of ω's possible values, as long as these prior probabilities are clearly stated in the experimental instructions. The experimenter only needs to measure the conditional beliefs $P^i_\omega(\cdot|I^i_\omega)$, for the different values of I^i_ω.

In other experiments, prior beliefs may be "homegrown" and do not relate one-to-one to a stylized set-up. For example, the beliefs may refer to real-world events. In these cases, the unconditional belief $P^i_\omega(\cdot)$ is harder to know but it can still be measured.

A similar methodological discussion to that in Question 1 applies here. The unconditional belief $P^i_\omega(\cdot)$ is best measured as the population-average belief, averaging over the values of I^i_ω. This method works irrespective of beliefs being homegrown or not.

For example, let ω be a binary event with values A and B. Information about this event may be homegrown in the sense that different participants have different knowledge about it even before the experiment begins. In addition, the experimenter can give half of the particpants a piece of information that is labelled "high" (which, let us say, indicates that $\omega = A$ is relatively likely) and give the other half a piece of information that is "low" (...unlikely). The population-average belief about A's likelihood is the desired "unconditional" belief $P^i_\omega(A)$: the midpoint between $P^i_\omega(A|\text{"high"})$ and $P^i_\omega(A|\text{"low"})$; both of them can be observed in the experiment.

A fully controlled environment (like balls from an urn) has the advantage that Bayes's rule gives analytic predictions for the beliefs' targets, i.e. for the true conditional probabilities. Question 2 can be applied directly to these benchmarks: is the updating from the signal too weak, relative to the Bayesian prediction? In contrast, an experiment that measures beliefs about naturally occuring events – and no Bayesian prediction – requires that the experimenter can sample the events sufficiently well to estimate their true distribution.

Experimental economists and cognitive psychologists have a long tradition of recording failures in the process of updating from new information. The evidence points to a particular stylized pattern: we update too much from small samples (or weak information), and too little from large samples (or strong information). In an early demonstration of this effect, Griffin and Tversky (1992) instruct their experimental participants that a particular coin is either biased by yielding 60% Heads and 40% Tails, or biased by yielding 60% Tails and 40% Heads. They also specify that the two possible biases occur with equal probability. In the experiment's main part, Griffin and Tversky show their participants sample throws of this coin and ask them to guess, conditional on a given sample, how likely it is that the coin is biased towards Heads. In cases where samples contain only few throws of the coin, the participants make guesses that are too extreme, i.e. too close to 0 or 1. For exam-

ple, if observing three throws that all land on Heads, the typical
response is to say that it is 85% certain that the coin is biased
towards Heads, whereas the true Bayesian posterior is only 77%.
In contrast, cases where the samples contain more throws induce
the participants to hold beliefs that are too close to the ex-ante
likelihood of one half. For example, if respondents observe that
11 out of 17 throws land on Heads, the typical assessment is that
it is 65% certain that the coin is biased towards Heads, whereas
the actual Bayesian posterior is 88%.

Question 3: Do we underappreciate the context when considering their action?

The third question combines the two previous ones. Do we use our information about the state of the world when predicting their actions?

We should certainly do so: their actions (including their statements) are far more predictable if we use our knowledge about the world.

This question covers the third and final conditional belief that arises before the conversation starts. Recall that only two aspects of uncertainty enter our utility directly, their action and the state of the world, and that we have two sets of information, about their type and about the state of the world. In principle, each of the two sets of information helps to predict each of the two aspects of uncertainty. This generates four conditional beliefs that are of interest. But by assumption, types are uncorrelated with the state of the world (see Chapter 2) and our information about their type is therefore not indicative about the state of the world. This leaves us with three relevant conditional beliefs.

Let us use a well-known term to re-phrase the question: do we appreciate the *common ground*? They and we live in the same world, we make similar experiences and obtain similar information. Do we account for this information sufficiently well when predicting their future behavior?

Appreciating the common ground sounds so easy. And yes, the common ground is very important for a good understanding of communication. But clearly, their information is different from our information. (How common is the ground?) Moreover, their inferences from their information may be hard for us to predict – and so may their actions.

This leads back to the distinction of things that we believe in, versus things that are only manifest to us. When predicting their actions, we need to ask what things *they* believe in, and what things are only manifest to them. We will enter this discussion in later chapters of this book. For now, the analysis's first step is to formulate a question without any mentalizing about their beliefs. Instead we consider our information – the things that are manifest to *us* – and ask how this information correlates with the actions of our partner in conversation. (We may happily observe that this is quite a simple question.)

As with the previous questions, we formulate a directed hypothesis: we may discriminate too little.

$$\text{Is } P^i_{a^j}(\cdot|I^i_\omega) \text{ too close to } P^i_{a^j}(\cdot)?$$

In the few seconds before the conversation with Ralph, Steve recognizes the context's exceptionality. Something is making Ralph very unhappy, to the extent that he effectively broke down in an empty street. Steve understands immediately that Ralph would hate to talk about what depresses him. He also understands that the context may induce a whole array of unusual actions of Ralph. On the one hand, Ralph may punish Steve for the intrusion. On the other hand, the revelation of his vulnerability may make Ralph relatively friendlier, softer, towards Steve. Overall, the context creates a wide set of utility consequences for Steve. He concludes that he must tread with care. We notice that this conclusion is fully consistent with the description of Ralph's possible types that appeared in Chapter 2. That is, Steve uses his information well, in light of this type description.

For Ralph, the dominant issue is his own acute problem. Before arriving at the scene, he had witnessed an act of domestic violence at his home, which he cannot forget. The fact that a smaller schoolkid, Steve, enters the scene is an additional disturbance. But it is difficult for Ralph to focus on the interaction with Steve and he does not know what to expect from it.

The flip side of using the state of the world to predict their action is to find a correct interpretation of a given action. Do we see their actions in context? This asks about attribution: do we view the person's type as the driver of their action, or do we view the context as the driver?

In many conversations, the answer is tricky because the context is endogenous. People choose their context, at least to some degree. Certain types are more likely to be found in certain contexts.

A key feature of experimental research comes in handy here: random role assignment. It guarantees that personal characteristics are uncorrelated with the context in which the participants find themselves in.

This feature creates a straightforward null hypothesis. In any experiment with random role assignment, how participants assess the personal characteristics of other participants should be independent of context and of the role that they take on.

The ''correspondence bias'' describes the tendency to attribute
the reasons and motivations of actions to the person committing
them, and not to the context. A classic experiment on the correspondence bias is by Ross et al. (1977) who ask pairs of participants to simulate a quizmaster situation. The two roles, quizmaster and contestant, are assigned to the participants at random,
at the beginning of the interaction. The quizmaster then asks the
contestant several quiz questions. In one condition of the experiment, CONTROL, the questions are taken from an existing set of
questions that were formulated by other quizmasters in previous
experimental sessions. In the TREATMENT condition, in contrast,
the quizmaster herself writes the questions during the present
session. In all sessions, quizmasters are under the instruction
that questions should be ''challenging but not impossible''. All
of this is known to the contestants. After the quizzes, both participants rate each other's level of general knowledge, on a scale
from 0 to 100. The main result is that in TREATMENT, where quizmasters write the questions themselves, the contestants judge the
quizmasters to be more knowledgable than themselves in 23 out of
24 pairs. Conversely, the quizmasters' ratings of the contestants
are balanced and 12 out of 24 quizmasters rate themselves higher
than the contestants, on average. In CONTROL, where the quizmasters do not formulate the questions themselves, such a balanced
result appears in both roles. Overall, only the constestants in
TREATMENT violate the null hypothesis of balanced assessments:
they believe that quizmasters are knowledgable because they come

up with difficult questions. On average, this is a false belief because the role of quizmaster is, as described above, chosen at random. The contestants' mistake is that they fail to incorporate the contextual information that the quizmasters are under the explicit instruction to formulate challenging questions.

Chapter 4

Talking

Now, at last, the actual conversation. This chapter describes how our beliefs may be off target when we talk. The difference to the previous chapter is that we now focus on their *reaction* to our statement.

Our beliefs about their reaction are, conveniently, the only bit of our beliefs that depends on what we say: there are three uncertain aspects (actions, issues, types) but we already know our type, we control our actions, and we cannot influence the state of the world or their type. Our success as talker depends, entirely, on how well we predict their reaction.

A widely held view of communication is that language is a convention. They and we have arrived, through our previous experiences or perhaps through some type of agreement, at a use of signals that allows information to be conveyed.

The key of such conventions is common interest: they and we *want* to communicate because it makes our utilities increase in unison. The talker wants the listener to learn something. Having learnt it, the listener does something that is good for both.

The common interest also fixes the beliefs about language use. The talker expects the listener to stick to the agreed language because doing so lies in the listener's interest. The listener expects the talker to do the same. The convention reinforces itself.

Or does it? The reasoning certainly opens a number of questions. What *is* the interest of our partner in conversation, and is it the same as ours? Are our beliefs really conventional, in the above sense of the word, and do

31

 https://doi.org/10.11647/OBP.0367.04

we agree which convention, out of many possible ones, we use? Do we really know what signals to use, and are these signals suitable for the present purpose? Is our language not far richer than what could possibly be agreed upon?

The book proceeds very slowly and seeks answers in small steps. It does not take any convention as given. Rather, it asks about the individual beliefs that, taken together, may or may not form a convention. As we will see, the interplay of beliefs is indeed far richer than what a convention can achieve.

Question 4: Do we predict a too-small reaction?

Even small steps are complex: notice that our talking is not only what we actually say in the circumstance that we find ourselves in, but also what we would have said in other circumstances. Our talking is a contingent plan. It depends on our type, it depends on what we know about the state of the world, and it depends on what we know about their, the other person's, type.

Our talking is informative because of this property: what we say in a given circumstance would not have been said in other circumstances.

Moreover, not only do we say something different in every circumstance but we could also have said many different things in the same circumstance. Checking whether or not our talking is optimal means checking for each circumstance whether or not the statement that we make gives us a higher utility than everything else that could be said.

The assumptions of Chapter 2 allow translating this into an empirical question in terms of our beliefs. Are they accurate?

We already observed that the other person's reaction is the only uncertain aspect that is moved by our talking. We therefore characterize our talking by our belief about how they react to our statements, in any given circumstance that we may be in.

Using the formal notation, the relevant belief of person i is $P^i_{a^j}(\cdot|\cdot)$. The first placeholder $\cdot$ holds the place for the possible values of person j's reaction a^j and the second $\cdot$ holds the place for the things that person i conditions on: her statement a^i and her circumstance, which is summarized by the information sets $I^i_{\theta j}$ and I^i_ω. (Knowledge of her own type, θ^i, is of course also part of person i's circumstance. The book leaves this out of the discussion, for brevity.)

We consider a whole collection of such conditional beliefs; one for each statement and circumstance. That is, the collection has one belief about a^j for each possible value of $(a^i, I^i_{\theta j}, I^i_\omega)$. This collection is called *person i's talking belief.*

(Later chapters will re-name it person i's *first-order* talking belief, but for now the brief version is fine.)

The question of accuracy, then, asks about the predictive power of our talking belief: is it close to the true probability distribution of their reaction, for each of our possible statements and circumstances? Accordingly, this chapter asks three directed questions about our talking belief, accounting for the fact that the belief changes with our statement, our information about their type, and our information about the state of the world.

The first question, Question 4, is the simplest and asks whether our beliefs respond too little to the possible statements that we could make: do we believe that they react less strongly than they actually do?

The opposite effect may be empirically true, too. Instead of under-estimating, we may over-estimate how strongly they react to our statement. They may decide not to answer us at all. We may mumble. They may not identify the words, or not have the capacity to process them. More generally, they and/or we may suffer from constraints in the transmission and if we tend to be unaware of this, then we may over-estimate their reaction. However, in parallel with the other questions in the book, we ask about a possible under-differentiation:

$$\text{Is } P^i_{a^j}(\cdot | a^i) \text{ too close to } P^i_{a^j}(\cdot)?$$

The action that Steve cares about is whether or not Ralph acts aggressively. Steve is quite pessimistic about this but expects that an offer to play ball makes it less likely that Ralph would express anger. Indeed, the push by Ralph, while unfriendly, is a good outcome for Steve. Ralph behaves in a way that one may call normal, for his standards. In contrast, a statement that enquires about Ralph's state of despair would plausibly have backfired. Steve's belief is accurate in predicting the direction in which his statement influences Ralph, perhaps even underestimating the size of the effect.

For the purpose of measurement, let us examine talking beliefs more closely. $P_{a^j}^i(\cdot|a^i)$ is a probability distribution (as subjectively expected by person i) over the actions that person j may pick in response to a^i. It is a different distribution for each possible a^i, and can be measured by asking simple questions. ("How likely is it that they react by choosing A if you say a^i?" – and similar questions for the other possible reactions of person j.)

These beliefs also depend on person i's circumstance ($I_{\theta j}^i$ and I_{ω}^i) but for now we can take the circumstance as given. If the experimenter wants to measure only the believed reaction to a^i but not its interaction with $I_{\theta j}^i$ and I_{ω}^i, then she can simply ignore them.

Parallel to the discussion in the previous chapter, a question arises: how can one measure the unconditional belief $P_{a^j}^i(\cdot)$?

The answer, also parallel to the discussion in the previous chapter, is that it is best to measure this unconditional belief as a weighted average of conditional beliefs. Specifically, the average of $P_{a^j}^i(\cdot|a^i)$, averaging over different statements a^i.

(This average belief is potentially very different from what we would expect person j to do in the absence of a statement. The very act of talking may make person j change their behavior and person i may anticipate this.)

So the experimenter aims to measure a weighted average of the collection $\{P_{a^j}^i(\cdot|a^i)\}_{a^i}$ – but with what weights? The problem is that most experimental studies, even if they fix the set of *possible* statements, do not impose the choice of a^i; it is chosen by person i. This renders it unclear how to weight the possible values of a^i in the aggregation.

Here in Chapter 4, we address this complication only for the simplified, binary case there are only two possible statements, $a^i \in \{A, B\}$, like in our discussions of Rachel, Dimitri and Steve. (Chapter 5 will discuss the more general case.) In the binary case, the weights of the possible values of a^i do not matter for answering Question 4, at least not for answering it in a qualitative way: any weighted average lies between the two conditional beliefs

$P_{a^j}^i(\cdot|A)$ and $P_{a^j}^i(\cdot|B)$, and the same is true for the empirical choice frequencies of person j that these beliefs refer to. The question can be thus answered by simply asking whether $P_{a^j}^i(\cdot|A)$ and $P_{a^j}^i(\cdot|B)$ are closer to each other than the corresponding choice frequencies of person j.

In any case, $P_{a^j}^i(\cdot|a^i)$ needs to be measured for each participant in the role of player i and each statement a^i, independent of whether or not the participant makes the statement. One can then piece the measurements together and compare them to the empirical reactions of person j, yielding the answer to Question 4.

A key feature of such an experiment is to have well-defined action spaces: the set of possible statements and the set of possible reactions. If both sets are small, a participant in the role of person i can report the entire family of talking beliefs.

The experimenter may also want to control the incentives of the participants, e.g., by paying money for given combinations of statements, reactions, and states of the world. This allows deriving predictions under standard assumptions about the participants' preferences. In particular, the experimenter can determine the game-theoretic equilibria as benchmarks for the analysis. Doing so may well be useful for the understanding of the data patterns – not least because the previously mentioned "conventions" are often described as game-theoretic equilibria, and the experimenter can use the belief data to test the equilibrium hypothesis.

This re-emphasizes, in passing, one of the book's main points: while the equilibrium requires all beliefs to be accurate, the book describes a more general approach where beliefs can be off target. The reader will see that many of the book's concepts are suitable for many possible beliefs.

A final note on conventions: different conventions are differently informative. For example, one can always agree to be entirely uninformative. After such an agreement, no-one will deviate: the listener does not react differently to different things that the talker may say. The talker knows this and may just as well say anything, with no relation to the circumstance. A self-fulfilling prophecy.

Game theorists call this uninformative convention a "babbling equilibrium". It is an extreme case. Many similar conventions, perhaps with small degrees of informativeness, may also apply.

But talking beliefs are relevant in every possible set-up: even if the situation is not so well-described, or if the theory is incomplete, or if its assumptions are invalid. Question 4 does not require an equilibrium analysis. It asks directly about the talking belief, wherever it may come from.

Sheremeta and Shields (2013) conduct an experiment that measures the talking belief in a minimal version of a salesman pitch. The talker knows the quality of a possible investment (good/bad) and indicates the quality to a listener who then decides about investing. The investment is binary and thus the situation is a simple sequential 2x2 game: the talker announces ''good'' or ''bad'' quality, the listener invests or not. If the quality is indeed good and the listener invests, she earns money in the experiment. If the quality is bad and she invests, she looses money. The talker, in contrast, earns money if and only if the listener invests, independent of quality. This creates an incentive to announce ''good'' quality even if quality is actually bad -- the non-alignment of incentives reduces the effective informativeness of the statements. (In this game, standard game theory predicts that only babbling equilibria exist.) The experiment also includes a belief elicitation task where the talker reports his talking belief: the probability with which he expects the listener to invest for each of the two possible statements (''good''/''bad''). The data show that the talking beliefs are quite accurate in this game, and that messages are viewed as informative. The averages of the talker's stated beliefs about whether or not the listener invests after hearing the ''good''/''bad'' message are 69% and 18%, whereas the actual investment rates in these cases are 67% and 15%, respectively. While the talkers' stated beliefs are spot-on, the question arises whether their quality announcements are consistent with the belief statements: for these beliefs, it is money-maximizing to always announce ''good'' quality. Do talkers' announcements show such a pattern? The answer is, only a mild majority of talkers show it: 60% of talkers are willing to lie, i.e. announce a ''good'' quality also in the case that the actual quality is bad. The remaining 40% of talkers are honest about a bad quality if it arises. A simple possible explanation is lying aversion, in the sense that the talker prefers to not announce ''good'' quality if this announcement does not match the truth. However, the effect of lying aversion would have to be

```
quite strong, perhaps implausibly strong, in order to explain the
highly frequent truthtelling: the elicited beliefs show that par-
ticipants expect honest behavior to be quite costly, shaving off a
substantial part of one's earnings. A complementary explanation,
for which Sheremeta and Shields (2013) find evidence with addi-
tional analyses, is that the talkers are ''ahead averse'' (on top
of being lying averse) in the sense of having a preference against
earning money at the expense of the listeners. Both explanations
are within the scope of assumptions in Chapter 2, corresponding
to specific utility functions uᵢ. Overall, this discussion il-
lustrates both caveats and advantages of measuring beliefs: the
elicitation of talking beliefs may not easily result in a defini-
tive explanation for observed talking behavior, but it can help
quantifying competing hypotheses.
```

Question 5: Do we underappreciate different people's differences in reacting?

Refining the previous question, we ask how our talking belief varies for different listeners. We should use our information about their type, as it is indicative of their reaction. If we were in their shoes, our reaction to a statement would clearly be person specific, wouldn't it? Only we, or someone very much like us, would react like we do; or so it seems to us. Well, we are not them and we therefore have to anticipate how they, in their own shoes, may react.

Doing so, we face an informational asymmetry. They know much more about themselves than we do. But we know at least something, on the basis of which we can discriminate (in the belief sense of the word).

A sophisticated belief considers what their different types *could be* and how each of them would react. The details of this conditional thinking depends on the conversation. In some conversations, we care only about how the average person reacts to what we say. In other conversations, we care about the entire set of reactions by different types.

This leads to the "art of questioning". We may want them to reveal their type. We may want them to say something that is specific to their preferences and restrictions. We may want to get them to talk.

It can be a good idea to ask an *open* question, i.e., one with a wide set of possible answers. Communication scholars have found that listeners often respond to such questions with relatively high frankness and accuracy. Another trick to find out about their type is to ask an *affective* question, i.e. one that addresses their emotions or personality traits directly.

Connecting the idea of open questions to the assumptions of Chapter 2, we note that the restriction of their possible answers is not a technical one. In most conversations, our statement does not literally make their set of possible reactions wider or narrower. (They are free to say whatever they want.) Rather, our statement influences the utility that they get from their different possible reactions. It thereby rules out, or rules in, some of their possible reactions.

A question that is open is, then, one that makes many of their possible reactions potentially beneficial for them. In this sense, openness is close to politeness. Using an expression from the linguistic literature, our statement is polite if it does not threaten their *negative face*: it does not diminish their freedom to make a decision at will.

All of this applies not only when we ask a question. It applies to any statement that we may make. We want to influence their possible reactions. How they react depends on our statement but also on their type. All the more reason for us to anticipate their type-specific reaction well.

$$\text{Is } P^i_{a^j}(\cdot|a^i, I^i_{\theta^j}) \text{ too close to } P^i_{a^j}(\cdot|a^i)?$$

Dimitri should have given Agniezka's type more thought. What if she dislikes engaging in conflict? Dimitri knows her too little to predict her next steps. In particular, it is natural to suspect that she may not react positively to his talk about future "blood". Moreover, Dimitri is impolite in that he pushes the question of the team's continuation. He implicitly pressures her to make a statement about it. Her inclination to continue the teamwork may have been more positive if he had simply said nothing.

Open questions – or other prompts for the other person to speak unrestrictedly – are difficult to deal with in an empirical analysis, exactly because of the lack of restrictions. The talker cannot report beliefs about the listener's possible reactions if the listener has too many of them available.

Instead of asking for talking beliefs directly, one may infer them indirectly, from the statements that a talker makes. The empirical strategy of the experimenter may be to ask, "What beliefs would justify these statements?"

This is, of course, precisely the empirical strategy that the book pursues all along. The question arises, then, whether we can pursue this question equally well, or perhaps even better, if we do not have belief reports but instead rely on indirect inference from the statements.

Such an inference certainly requires assumptions about the connection between statements and beliefs. But this alone makes no big difference: recall Chapter 2, arguing that we need to make such assumptions even if we measure beliefs directly by asking for reports (we may need pretty much the same assumptions for both methods, actually).

What else, then, speaks to the methodological question whether it is better to infer beliefs or to ask for belief reports?

On the one hand, asking for belief reports can be costly and intrusive. Costly because their measurement requires an elaborate survey. Intrusive because the measurement itself may change the observation – it imposes a machinery on the conversation. The interlocutors, when facing the task of belief elicitation, are not in their natural habitats any more. This may affect their way of communicating, or it may affect their beliefs.

On the other hand, as described, a disadvantage of inferring beliefs is that the action spaces are often too large. Analyses of free-flowing conversations are likely to be underdetermined. Too many things could be said by the talker, and for each of them, too many possible expectations about the listener's reactions can provide possible reasons for what is said. The analyst has too many degrees of freedom.

As a feasible way out of the problem of having too-large action spaces, one can artificially limit the scope of the conversation ex post, by classifying the available statements into a small set of categories. An ex-post text analysis can thereby transform the statements into a suitable data set that describes the talker's choice set in a simplified way. It is unlikely, however, that the interlocuters converse with the same classification in mind. The method therefore carries the baggage of additional, and unrealistic, assumptions.

Overall, from the experimenter's perspective, allowing a free-flowing conversation and inferring underlying talking beliefs is a possible option, but an imperfect one.

Let us ask this methodological question differently: if we ask for a belief report, is this really the belief that we are interested in? Are the 18 questions of this book not rather aimed at a set of latent beliefs that underlie the choices and statements – what economists call *revealed expectations*?

The answer is that we are indeed interested in these latent beliefs, first and foremost. The elicitation of belief reports only gives an incomplete proxy for latent beliefs. It may or may not be the best available proxy. It, too, is a possible-but-imperfect option. The analyst, when choosing the method, should weigh the pros and cons. This book, aiming for precision in the experimental set-up, makes a choice by largely focusing on the technique of direct elicitation. But the choice is not meant to be definitive about what is the best method.

A final remark on method, especially for the purpose of answering Question 5: one also needs measures of the dependence on $I_{\theta j}^i$. This requires observations for different sets of listeners. As a variation of the methods in Chapter 3, one can describe several hypothetical vignettes to the talker, each of which ask her to imagine a different identity of the listener. The experimenter can then measure whether the (elicited or inferred) talking beliefs react to the information about the listener.

Partial and indirect evidence on Question 5 appears in the empirical literature on politeness. Holtgraves and Yang (1990) take a middle ground in terms of restricting statements: they pre-fix a set of statements and ask the participants to assess the statements in terms of how likely they would use each of them in a given situation. These assessment have a fairly clear interpretation in terms of talking beliefs: judging a statement to be likely to be used indicates that one also judges the statement as fulfilling the goals of the talker's aim better than a less-likely-to-be-used statement. (The reader may dispute this assumption, but let us take it as given.) Holtgraves and Yang's study also lets the identity of the listener vary, by describing the situation as a

pair of vignettes with two different co-workers: one in which
the talker and the listener are close to each other, here named
Treatment CLOSE, versus one where talker and listener have a more
distant relationship (Treatment DISTANT). Moreover, an important
part of the research design is that the statements reflect different levels of politeness, ranging from bold (e.g., ``Go get the
mail'') to a more polite, indirect request (e.g. ``Has the mail
arrived yet?''). The results of the experiment show that impolite
requests are believed to be significantly more likely to be chosen in CLOSE than in DISTANT, and in the opposite order for polite
requests (but insignificantly so). On a scale from 1 to 7, the participants assess an impolite request to be chosen with an average
likelihood score of 2.62 in CLOSE, versus 2.38 in DISTANT; a polite request is judged to have likelihood scores of 4.43 in CLOSE
and 4.54 in DISTANT. This indicates that talking beliefs differ
depending on the information about the listener. Whether the differentiation is sufficiently large, given how listeners actually
behave, cannot be judged from this experiment.

Question 6: Do we forget about the world when predicting their reaction?

As indicated in Chapter 2, talking is not only about information. When we talk, we perform. Our statement is an action and it changes the world (a little bit) and certainly our utility.

Linguists and philosophers of language differentiate types of *speech acts*. For instance, a statement about the world is an assertive speech act. Such an assertive speech act is usually not meant to change the world directly. It only conveys information.

A direct influence on the world can be achieved through a declarative speech act like the governor's utterance that "here and now, we have to move on", which ends the conversation. A declarative speech act, if made appropriately, changes the world only by virtue of being made.

So what is the state of the world, and what is it not? In Chapter 2, ω was introduced as the collection of things that the people in the conversation cannot influence. But person i's statement a^i is chosen by her. How is all this consistent with the previous paragraph, which asserts that a statement can influence the state of the world?

The resolution of this little puzzle is that ω is unaffected by i's *present* statement. For any subsequent statement, in contrast, the present statement will already belong to the description of the state of the world, i.e., it will be part of the new ω.

Our analysis, thus, does not differentiate between assertive speech acts and declarative speech acts – in either case a^i cannot affect the state ω that is relevant for the present statement but it does affect the state that is relevant for the next step in the conversation. (This is just a technical observation about this book's analysis. The reader may nevertheless find it helpful to differentiate the different kinds of acts.)

All statements share the property that when we make them, we need to anticipate the other person's reaction. To do this well, we use our information about the context, I_ω^i. Has something relevant been said at an earlier stage? Are they, the other person, in a position to hear and process our statement? Did we make any other experience or observation that helps to predict their reaction?

This shows that the previously-mentioned "conventions" are misleading, or incomplete at best: no convention can cover all contexts. The talker knows this and anticipates a (non-conventional) context-dependent reaction.

Later chapters of the book will focus on how the listener's interpretation, and the talker's anticipation of this interpretation, may incorporate context information. But even now, we can already observe one important element of the reasoning: the listener's incentives to react change with ω, and the talker knows it.

More precisely, when person i talks, she knows that person j's utility reacts to ω and that his information about it will therefore influence his reaction. Given that i's information about ω is correlated with j's, i can use I_ω^i in her prediction about how j will react. The challenge is to do this in the right direction and to the right extent.

The discussion leads to the definition of person i's *perceived relevance* of information I_ω^i. This is i's expectation about the utility increase that she herself obtains from taking I_ω^i into account in her own talking.

(For precision, the sentences in these parentheses express the definition more formally: Fix i's belief about the reaction of j, $P_{a^j}^i(\cdot|\cdot, I_\omega^i)$, and first consider the statement that she finds optimal if using this belief – call it $\bar{a}^i$. Now consider what statement she would find optimal if she did not have the information, i.e. if her belief was $P_{a^j}^i(\cdot|\cdot)$, and call this statement $\bar{\bar{a}}^i$. This alternative action will lead to a different utility level. If person i compares the utilities from using the two statements, she will evaluate them with her actual belief in mind, $P_{a^j}^i(\cdot|\cdot, I_\omega^i)$. The perceived relevance of the information is, therefore, the difference in indirect utility that she expects to get from making statement $\bar{a}^i$ instead of $\bar{\bar{a}}^i$, using belief $P_{a^j}^i(\cdot|\cdot, I_\omega^i)$ in these expectations.)

An information is, thus, perceived relevant for person i if she thinks that she increases her utility by paying attention to it and making her statement accordingly. For later use, notice how this definition uses person i's belief about person j's reaction – she expects that he will react in a particular way – but that the definition does not use person j's information or his beliefs.

Notice also that this definition uses person i's *subjective* beliefs, when evaluating the utility difference that relates to an information about ω. Her belief P^i may, of course, be wrong in many ways – the relevance of I_ω^i is only perceived. But it is straightforward to also define an objective counterpart: one may consider how much her utility actually increases from paying optimal attention to the information, anticipating the true distribution of j's behavior.

One may call this utility difference the objective relevance of the information and, under this nomenclature, Question 6 asks whether the perceived relevance is close to the objective relevance of a given information. However, while these are all useful concepts, they are not easily measurable: utility differences cannot be elicited without a large machinery. It is easier, and consistent with the general notation in the book, if we formulate the question in terms of beliefs:

$$\text{Is } P_{a^j}^i(\cdot|a^i, I_\omega^i) \text{ too close to } P_{a^j}^i(\cdot|a^i)?$$

Rachel is surprised by the fact that the governor does not make even a half-decent commitment to follow up on her request for support. In her view, she puts forward a convincing statement about the state of the world, and he sits still. Rachel's misunderstanding is that while she finds the scientific state of knowledge about provenance decisive for what is the right course of action, the governor does not generally follow the science. For him, it is a political issue, not a scientific one. The relevance of the scientific truth of the findings is not objective, for this conversation.

To answer this question in an experiment, it is usually best to assign the relevant context information exogenously. (It avoids selection.) The experimenter may, for instance, describe the entire information structure to the participants: that there exist certain states of the world, each of which presents different incentives to the interlocutors, and how the uncertainty about the state of the world is resolved.

In particular, the participants acting in the role of the talker should not only observe their own signals about the state of the world, but they should also learn about how the information structure creates signals for the listener, i.e., what the listener may learn.

The ''Dictator Game'' has only one active player, the dictator, who chooses the size of a donation that she makes to the other player, the recipient. That's it -- the game is rather simple and this is good for the experimenter: the donation size serves as a straightforward measurement of generosity. The drivers of generosity can then be investigated in variants of the game, e.g., by including pre-play communication in the form of a binding suggestion: a third player, the talker, makes a suggestion to the dictator (the listener) about how much money to donate. The dictator first listens to the talker's suggestion and then either accepts or rejects it. Peltzer (2019) played this game under two conditions: a donation is either not very effective, meaning that the recipient receives exactly the donation amount that is given by the dictator, or it is very effective, in which case the recipient receives the donation amount multiplied by 3. The effectiveness is the state of the world. A signal about the state of the world is given to both the talker and the dictator: if the donation is not very effective, both of them receive a red signal with 0.75 probability and a green signal with 0.25 probability (the same signal for both, which is commonly known). Conversely, if the donation is very effective, both of them receive the green signal with 0.75 probability and the red signal with the remaining 0.25 probabil-

ity. The experiment measures talking beliefs by asking what the
talker expects about the probabilities of the dictator accepting
each of three different suggestions (EUR 2, EUR 4 and EUR 6, in each
case out of a maximum donation budget of EUR 8), conditional on the
signal being red or green. The experimenter can thus observe how
talking beliefs change with the information about the state of the
world. The results show how the dictator's reaction to the suggestion does indeed depend on the signal: with a green signal, the
acceptance probability is above one half for each possible suggestion, but with a red signal, the acceptance probability ranges
from about one quarter for the suggestion of EUR 6 to almost three
quarters for a suggestion of EUR 2. The talkers, however, underestimate the signal's influence on the dictator's acceptance: they
believe that with a green signal, the dictators would show a similar reaction to the case of a red signal -- e.g., that they accept
a suggestion of donating EUR 2 only one third of the time.

Chapter 5

Listening

Through listening, we update our beliefs about two utility-relevant aspects of uncertainty: the other person's future actions and the state of the world. Both co-vary with the other person's statement. If we listen well, we can understand what the statement indicates about the two unknowns. This chapter deals with different ways in which the updating may be inaccurate.

The chapter formulates each of its questions only once although it can be asked in two variants, one of them about the other person's future actions and the other about the state of the world. The two variants are fully analogous and it therefore suffices to ask each question only once.

Question 7: Do we listen too little?

The previous chapter illustrated how our talking is a contingent plan. When in the role of the talker, we say something under a specific circumstance and we say something else under another circumstance. We know that they, when in the role of the talker, do the same.

That is, our interpretation of their statement follows the logic of a language. What would they say if their circumstance was X and what if their circumstance was Y? (And so forth.) With a language in mind, and hearing what they actually say, we learn about the circumstance that they are in.

At least, we do so in theory. What we actually learn is an empirical question about our beliefs, just like all the other questions in this book. Other chapters of the book ask in more depth why they say what they say. This chapter contributes something more superficial but nonetheless important:

https://doi.org/10.11647/OBP.0367.05

it asks directly – in the sense of: at face value, without a deep interpretation – how our belief changes when we hear their statement.

This is *our listening belief*: for each of the two relevant uncertain aspects (their future actions and the state of the world), for each possible statement that they may make, and for each circumstance that we may be in, it specifies our belief about the aspect, conditional on hearing the statement.

As before, the focus lies on conditional probabilities; here, the conditionality refers to their statements and to our circumstance. This is a pretty large set of conditions – there are many, many combinations of possible statements and circumstances and, no doubt, our listening belief is therefore inaccurate. We cannot ever precisely guess a large set of numbers. But not every inaccuracy is equally important. What we care about is whether our listening belief is on target in the relevant dimensions of uncertainty: the dimensions that allow us to increase our utility through optimal reactions. For example, we may only be interested in predicting a particular future action of theirs, but not everything else that they might do or say.

Actually, we have many good excuses for updating badly when hearing their statement. One such excuse is that their statement is not our only input. In a sea of information that is manifest to us, a single statement's significance is easy to miss.

We must, however, not ignore the sea of information. Even if we find most of it uninteresting per se, it may be relevant for the interpretation of the statement. Questions 8 and 9 describe ways in which we may mis-judge the circumstance of the statement. The present question asks only about how much we condition on the statement itself.

An especially easy-to-miss element is that the talker may have had the *choice* to talk. As mentioned in earlier chapters, their statement carries a different meaning depending on whether they could have chosen to say nothing.

This caveat cuts both ways. If we observe that they do not say anything, we may update from this observation. Conversely, if we observe that they do say something, then we may update from this fact alone. We may, in particular, believe that the fact that they talk is indicative of the relevance of what they have to say.

The same logic applies to the choice of topic that they do, or do not, talk about. If we notice that they avoid a certain topic, this may inform us about this very topic. Conversely, if they do address a certain topic, then we may regard it as especially relevant and update our belief about it more than about other things.

An important formality is that listening beliefs are different in nature from talking beliefs: they relate to different uncertain aspects. Talking beliefs are about the other person's reaction to our statements. Listening beliefs are about what they do after their statement and about the state of the world. We therefore cannot compare the two sets of beliefs with each other. When measuring them, we determine their accuracy by comparing each of them to its own target, i.e., the actual probability (or frequency) that it refers to.

Finally, another note on notation: here and in the formulation of Questions 8 and 9, the symbol x stands in for either of the two unknown aspects of uncertainty $\{\omega, \tilde{a}^j\}$: ω is the state of the world and $\tilde{a}^j$ is the future action of person j, which is still uncertain after j said a^j.

Is $P_x^i(\cdot|a^j)$ too close to $P_x^i(\cdot)$?

Agniezka listens carefully to Dimitri and tries to assess his future actions. He had drawn her into this project, to form a team. Now, he is talking about "blood" and the question arises whose blood it is that he refers to. Would she, Agniezka, be in harm's way if she continues to be on the team, more than if she leaves the team? A noteworthy aspect of Dimitri's statement is that he does not imply in any way that he will blame her if she withdraws from the project now.

Measuring listening beliefs is tricky business. A talker makes only one statement. The listening belief, however, includes the posterior beliefs after every possible statement.

Once they have heard the statement, it would be difficult to ask the experimental participants about their belief for the counterfactual case that the talker would have said something else. It may therefore be better to ask for the listeners' conditional belief reports before the talker talks: what they believe in case that the talker makes one possible statement, likewise for the next possible statement, etc.

Another difficulty, a variant of which came up in Chapter 4, is that it is unclear how to compare the talking belief to its corresponding unconditional belief. What is $P_x^i(\cdot)$? Surely it is a weighted average of the conditional beliefs $P_x^i(\cdot|a^j)$, for different values of a^j – but with what weights?

In Chapter 4, we answered an analogous question only for the binary case of a statement that is either A or B. Now, we consider a more complete answer for the case of a multi-valued statement, in two steps. First, an abstract answer that works fine in theory – but requires a lot of data. Second, we consider how a realistic experiment would deal with this case.

The first, abstract answer is actually quite simple: simply weight each value of a^j by the frequency with which it occurs. In a large experiment with many participants in the role of person j, these frequencies are readily available: the experimenter observes the distribution of chosen statements. He or she can thus use these frequencies as weights to calculate both the belief $P_x^i(\cdot)$ and its target (the unconditional distribution of the unknown x that the belief is about). We note that this set of weights is appropriate in the sense of payoff relevance: the frequencies reflect the actual importance of each statement for person i's utility.

The second observation is about the practical implementation. Here, things are more difficult. If a^j has many possible values, then the data set must be so large that for every single one of these values, there are sufficiently many observations to estimate the average conditional belief with high precision. Otherwise, some of the conditional frequencies cannot be trusted and one may need advanced statistical methods to account for this sampling error.

Moreover, the expresssion "too close to", which describes a comparison of probability/frequency distributions, is perhaps too vague for a large set of values for a^j. If the experimenter is really interested in a large set of such values, then he or she may also be interested in some specific comparison of the relevant distributions and the expresssion "too close to" may not capture this well.

In actual practice, an experimenter will therefore likely proceed as in Chapter 4: if he or she can rely on the simplification that person j makes a binary statement that is either A or B, then the experimenter will do so and answer Question 7 (like Questions 4, 5, and 6) in a simple way. For a binary statement, the question boils down to asking whether $P_x^i(\cdot|A)$ is closer to $P_x^i(\cdot|B)$ than the corresponding actual distributions of x.

Importantly, an *ex-post* binarization is possible for experiments with a large set of possible statements: the experimenter may classify each of them into A or B, thereby enabling an analysis that is equivalent to the case where only these two statements exist.

Many statements amount to being a promise, or other announcement of one's own future behavior. Charness and Dufwenberg (2006) conduct an experimental game similar to the Trust Game that was described in Chapter 3 but with the additional feature that one player can make a promise, thereby potentially enticing the other player to trust him. A promise works as follows in this particular study. The second player announces that, if trusted, he will roll a die whose (random) outcome determines a monetary payment to the first player -- and payoff rules are such that if the second player actually rolls the die, then it is highly likely that the first player benefits from it. But the announcement is non-binding, i.e., the second player does not have to actually roll the die. The first player hears the announcement and her task is to decide whether to end the game early and thereby earn a low but safe payment, or to trust the second player and let him make the decision of rolling versus not rolling the die. The game also involves payments to the second player that give him an incentive to mislead the first player: if she trusts him, his payment increases and he can increase it even further by deviating from the promise and choosing not to roll the die. The experimental instructions are clear about the fact that the second player is obliged to say something, and the experimenters can classify the statements that the participants make into two categories, those that effectively promise the friendly ''I will roll'' versus those that do not do so, which we may understand as announcing ''I won't roll''. The data show that participants who promise ''I will roll' are indeed much more likely to actually roll the die. The respective frequencies of rolling are 79% for the participants who promise ''I will roll'' versus 33% for those who do not promise it. But when participants acting as first players are asked what they believe about the probability of rolling after hearing the statement, they reveal listening beliefs that do not discriminate enough: the reported average expectations of actual rolling after hearing statements ''I will roll'' and ''I won't roll'' are 64% and 51%, respectively.

Question 8: Do we underdifferentiate talkers?

We form our expectations based not only on what they say, but also on who they are. The same statement, when uttered by different people, means different things. We therefore condition our listening belief on our information about their type.

When predicting their future actions, two effects arise that require such differentiation of talkers. First, different types do different things in the future, and second, different types make different announcements (and then do different things in the future).

When predicting the state of the world, the first of these effects is irrelevant but the second effect remains valid: different types say different things. We therefore learn in a type-dependent way from their statements.

A possible complication is that we may also learn something important *about* their type when we hear their statement. They say something and we may realize that our prior belief about their type was wrong. Why should we, then, condition on our prior information?

The answer is that we should use all information. Neither should we condition only on the prior information nor should we use only the new information that the statement contains. The relevant belief is a posterior belief – forming it well requires that we use our prior belief, but with good measure.

This requires a good meta-accuracy about our prior. If we are too certain about their type, then our interpretation of the statement may suffer. Likewise, if we give too little weight to our prior view of their type, then our posterior is inaccurate, too. We may, e.g., enage in too much temporal extension, meaning that we overgeneralize the momentary impression that we receive from the present statement.

Recall also that we do not care about their type per se. Chapter 2 ruled it out by assumption. Assessing their type is important to us only because it helps us learn.

This is a good moment for pause. *Why* does our listening belief depend on our information about their type?

A very rational reason is that their type describes their incentives. We anticipate that they choose their statement optimally, from their perspective. For instance, they may want us to learn something. They may also simply enjoy saying what they say.

Recall our slow, piecemeal approach: this chapter does not yet consider the other person's perspective in any detail. Presently, we only recognize that different types will choose different statements. This may indeed have to do with their incentives, in a large number of ways. Yet, it may also stem from less sophisticated reasons. We may be differently perceptive with different people. We may attribute a different degree of informativeness to them, for reasons other than incentives (including prejudices). We may be in a different mood depending on who is the talker. Knowing who they are may make us more, or less, curious about what they have to say. The information may mislead us by installing an *idée fixe* about their future actions or the state of the world. In any case, our listening belief varies, for rational or irrational reasons, with what we know about the talker.

The discussion of Question 6 included a definition of the perceived relevance of an information that person i has. This was in the context of person i being the talker, and the information was about the state of the world. Here, for Question 8, we notice that the concept of perceived relevance also applies to person i being the listener (not the talker) and to cases where the relevant information is about the other person's type (not the state of the world). We skip over the technical specifications of all these variations of relevance – they would be fully analogous to the one in Question 6 – and merely remark on the generality of the concept: perceived relevance may apply for the talker and for the listener, and for all kinds of information. All variants of perceived relevance will also be important later, in the second half of the book where we will ask about the interlocutors' beliefs about what is relevant from the perspective of the other interlocutor.

To summarize the discussion of type-specific listening: in the case of person i being the listener who has information $I^i_{\theta j}$, the information is potentially relevant because it helps her to anticipate better the subsequent action of person j and/or to better update about the state of the world. The empirical question is whether she does it to the right extent, which we express – as usual – in a directed question about her beliefs.

$$\text{Is } P^i_x(\cdot|a^j, I^i_{\theta j}) \text{ too close to } P^i_x(\cdot|a^j)?$$

The governor listens well enough to put an end to the discussion; he understands that he can proceed in the meeting by giving praise to Rachel, strong but vague, not promising her anything. He does not notice, however, the possible significance of scientific research about the provenance of art collectibles. Rachel's remark about it establishes certain facts (she is a scientist, after all) and implies the possibility that these facts may have relevant political consequences. Yet, the governor only refers to other issues.

In other words, he has a sophisticated updating about future actions and the state of the world on those dimensions that he was prepared for: Rachel as a political stakeholder who may ask for funds. He fails to engage with her expertise, and therefore with the information that is new to him.

How can an experiment create a meaningful variation in person i's information about person j's type? Most populations of experimental participants are quite homogeneous. For example, university students are all of similar age and educational status. Highlighting the differences between them requires some effort. Moreover, the highlighting itself may distort the measurement. The experimental participants may pay attention to things that they would otherwise not pay attention to – an instance of "experimenter demand", meaning that the participants react to what they believe is the purpose of the experiment.

One possibility is to use an existing set of statements that were uttered by a heterogeneous pool of people in a different environment and that were recorded with a different purpose.

Belot et al. (2012) report on an experiment using video material taken from a TV game show. Participants in a decision laboratory watch actual episodes of a show where the contestants play a simple game of cooperation: two contestants simultaneously decide to either cooperate or not, with monetary rewards. Each player has a unilateral incentive to avoid cooperation but earns far more if the other player cooperates. Before the cooperation game commences, the game show contestants can talk to each other. They use this pre-play communication phase to make announcements about their future cooperation -- which may induce the other person to cooperate, too. In the decision laboratory, the video screening stops after the communication phase and the experimental participants are asked to report their beliefs about whether or not the contestant whose statements they have heard will actually cooperate. The pool of contestants contains people with many different characteristics, at least one of which is known to the experimental participants: gender. The lab participants should therefore condition on the contestant's gender in their interpretations of what they hear. They do so, but too little. While promises made by women are more predictive of cooperation than promises made by men by a difference of 19 percentage points, the lab participants only predict a difference in predictiveness of eight percentage points.

Question 9: Are we too impressionable?

A discussion similar to that in Question 8 applies to our use of manifest information about the world – the context. We know something before they say something. We have to put the two together. Do we condition on context to the right extent?

We condition on context for three reasons. First, their talking strategy differs for different contexts. Second, for a given strategy on their side, we update about the state of the world differently for different contexts – because we have different prior beliefs about it. Third, we also update differently about their future actions – we expect them to be context-dependent in addition to the possibility that statements are context-dependent.

The first of these considerations highlights that we need to investigate the mind of the talker. Just as we use our knowledge, they use theirs, too. Our information is not the same as their information but it is indicative of it and we may thus appreciate the context in which they talk. The next chapters will continue this thread.

The second and third consideration takes the talker's talking strategy as given and focusses on how we interpret it. Our information about the world may help us to see that their statement makes certain states of the world, or certain future actions, more or less plausible.

All of these considerations can be expressed by a single question about our own listening belief: does it react well to our knowledge about the state of the world? Just as all previous questions, it is an empirical question whose answer does not require a full understanding of underlying mechanisms. The statement that we hear has a certain statistical informativeness and it is in our interest to recognize this informativeness as accurately as possible.

Challenges arise, once again, from the multitude of dimensions: what parts of the context are we aware of, and to which of them does our listening belief react? Or, to use the term relevance again: what context information is perceived relevant for us as listener?

A feature may help here: that we hear their statement and can reconsider the context's relevance in light of the statement. That is, we may listen to their statement not only by updating about the state of the world, but also by shifting our attention to a new background.

We may, however, still neglect the objectively relevant parts of the context. For instance, we may be overly impressed by what they say. Their statement may come with a lot of eloquence, evidence, or other persuasive force.

$$\text{Is } P_x^i(\cdot|a^j, I_\omega^i) \text{ too close to } P_x^i(\cdot|a^j)?$$

Ralph's listening is naive. He accepts all-too-easily that the possibility of a ball game is the relevant topic. (Perhaps understandably so – recall that Steve carries a ball, which is a visible cue.) Ralph misses what else Steve could have addressed and what would have been far more relevant, namely Ralph's state of despair. Interpreting this context as the topic of conversation and showing a violent reaction to Steve's statement – or, more gently, telling a cover-up story – may have enabled Ralph to better defend his position in the schoolyard pecking order.

Making monetary payments as part of the experiment is commonly done in experimental economics but not so in experiments of other fields. Why is that?

An ill-meaning explanation is that economists are money fetishists. They regard money as an important motivator, whereas other scholars do not. A less ill-meaning explanation is that economists want maximum control over the experiment. They prefer to restrict attention to an analysis where one dimension is well understood and controlled, even if other dimensions are left out.

This is no coincidence. The thinking of economists often follows their leading theory of decision making, expected utility theory, which describes utility as a one-dimensional real number. Money is one-dimensional, too, which is part of why economists like to analyze it.

In this book we use the same simplification. Recall the payoff mapping introduced in Chapter 2, $u^i : A^i \times A^j \times \Omega \times \Theta^i \to \mathbb{R}$; it is important that u^i is a one-dimensional summary of person i's welfare, about which we can assume that person i maximizes its expected value.

(The maximization may be misguided because person i's beliefs are subjective, i.e., potentially false. This is the whole point of the book. Notice that this point, too, could not be made equally well if we did not assume that person i maximizes u^i given her belief.)

u^i is not money, though. It is the utility that a person receives from a combination of the realized values of the three uncertain aspects. The mapping u^i can take on many forms and the analysis works under a whole range of different assumptions about it. For instance, economists sometimes suppose for simplicity that u^i is a linear scaling of person i's own money payments. In this case, the earnings of others, and the risk arising from the variability in the uncertain aspects, do not bother person i. She is selfish and risk neutral. Alternatively, the utility u^i could be assumed to be a nonlinear transformation of money. This allows capturing risk preferences. Or, u^i could depend on person j's payments as well, which would capture social preferences.

The experimenter may make monetary payments not only for the actions (or statements) in the experiment, but also for the participants' belief reports. The experimenter can thereby give appropriate incentives to give honest reports.

Paying for belief reports – how does this work? Imagine that person i is asked to predict a binary action of person j, $\tilde{a}^j \in \{A, B\}$. Then person i's belief about this action is a number between zero and one – the probability that $\tilde{a}^j = A$. Incentivizing the belief report amounts to paying money such that person i maximizes her expected utility if she reports her true belief.

A simple mechanism achieves this: person i receives a fixed payment F with a probability that decreases quadratically in the distance between her reported belief and the ex-post realized truth state of A (which is 1 if person

j chooses A, and 0 otherwise). That is, if person j actually chooses A and person i predicted that this would happen with probability r, then she earns F with probability $1 - (1 - r)^2$. If, on the other hand, person j actually chooses B then person i receives F with probability $1 - r^2$.

This mechanism has the property that reporting one's (subjective) expectation of j's behavior is the optimal response for person i, no matter what her risk preferences are. Other, simpler mechanisms have other theoretical properties. E.g. if the reward that a participant gets for her belief report decreases linearly in its distance from the truth, then the mechanism makes it optimal for person i to report the median of her subjective distribution.

Most participants will likely find the exact version of the monetary incentives not too important. Indeed, there is very little evidence in the literature that the exact rule matters, given that an experiment rewards accuracy in one way or another. There is, however, some evidence that it matters (mildly) whether one uses monetary rewards at all. The belief reports have been shown to discriminate better and be more consistent with one's own actions if money is paid.

Eyster et al. (2018) run experiments where people sometimes forget their prior beliefs and react to other people's statements far too much -- they are too impressionable. A large group of participants listen to each others' statements, where each statement is an estimate of a sum of numbers. The participants act in sequence, after each of them was endowed with a privately known number that is randomly drawn from a mean-zero distribution. When called upon to make her statement, a participant's goal is to guess the sum of all privately-known numbers of the participants who appeared previously in the sequence, including her own number. She reports her guess of this ''target'' and is rewarded for accuracy: her monetary reward decreases (here, linearly) in the distance between the guess and the true sum of numbers, calculated up to her own position in the game. The game-theoretic, rational prediction is that everyone hits the target and earns the full payoff: since all guesses are public, later participants can use the previous guesses to infer what underlying numbers each of the previous participants must have seen. If they figure the previous numbers out, they can add their own number to it. But figuring out the previous numbers may be difficult. In one treatment, participants announce their guesses one after the other, in a slow and transparent manner. Each person's best guess is, here, simply to add one's own number to the previous guess. Participants are mostly successful in tracking the correct sum of numbers in this way. They, however, mildly over-react to previous participants' guesses, and would earn more on average by shading their guess towards the ex-ante expected value of their target (which is zero) by roughly one third. In a second treatment, participants act in lumps. At each point in time, four participants have to announce their guesses. This makes the learning process more complicated as one cannot simply add one's number to the previous guess. (The game-theoretic prediction still uses simple arithmetics, but in a lengthy way.) Participants make systematic mistakes in this treatment, by following the direction of previous guesses to an extreme extent. Early guesses are incorporated again and again, with far too much weight: they are, effectively, multiple-counted, leading everyone's guesses to go far astray. On average, participants should move closer to the target's ex-ante expected value by no less than 98% in this treatment. The effect is so strong that participants who act in the second half of this treatment would earn twice as much money in the experiment if they were to ignore all previous guesses and simply reported only their own numbers.

Chapter 6

Seeing what they don't see

Now we turn the table, and mentalize. We consider *their* view of the conversation and ask about their expectations. It is the book's main trick: we dig deeper by re-asking everything that has been asked before, but now about our view of the other side of the table.

The book therefore returns to square one and first considers the initial perspective – about the conversation before it even starts. What do they know when they enter the conversation, and what would they like to know?

The answer is that they know neither our actions nor the state of the world, and that they would like to know both. (So that they can pick a better action.) They will therefore consider their information about our type, which helps them to predict our action, and they will consider their information about the state of the world, which helps them to predict both of their unknowns.

Does our mentalizing reflect this?

The problem has two layers. The inner layer is that we need to form beliefs about their beliefs, in order to understand their view on the conversation. These second-order beliefs are the basis for the outer layer, which consists of our first-order beliefs about the things that *we* care about: their actions and the state of the world. The first-order beliefs are the basis for our actions and statements.

Here is the good news: the previous chapters have already dealt with the outer layer. They already asked what biases of our first-order beliefs may be prevalent and detectable.

61

 https://doi.org/10.11647/OBP.0367.06

As discussed earlier, the previous chapters asked all of these questions as empirical questions and did not go any further. They did not ask for the reasons of the biases, which we do now at least to some extent: if the inner layer – our beliefs about their beliefs – is off target, it can explain why the outer layer – our beliefs – is off target, too.

(Notice, here we go on re-naming: The talking beliefs and listening beliefs of the previous chapters are subsequently called *first-order talking beliefs* and *first-order listening beliefs*.)

Question 10: Do we fail to see ourselves in the mirror?

They do not know our type and therefore cannot predict our statements and actions. They cannot read our minds and cannot know our fears and desires. They have some information about all of it; luckily, much less than we do.

These are obvious facts but it is less obvious how well we factor them in. A first obstacle is that we may fail to know what information they may have about us. A second obstacle is that we may mis-interpret how they use their information. We may fail to understand how they, given what is manifest to them, predict our actions.

Ugh, what a messy, two-headed insufficiency: our knowledge is imperfect and, on top of it, our way of dealing with it is imperfect. To make things simple, the book only deals with the second obstacle. How is information used? In the case of the present question: how do we think that they use their information about our type?

(Thinking back to the previous chapters, we note that they, too, were all about the second type of obstacle. Nowhere in these chapters did we ask whether, how, or why the information that we have may be wrong. Of course it may indeed be wrong; but this is for another book.)

The first question about second-order beliefs, Question 10, asks whether we believe their belief about our actions to condition too little on their information about our type. That we may think of them as not using their information as much as they actually do. Or, the opposite bias, that we

think of them as using it more than they do. More generally, that we fail to
see the degree to which they look at a conversation with us as being different
from a conversation with someone else.

Expressed in the previous chapters' words: do we think that they do not
discriminate well? Do we overestimate or underestimate the extent to which
Question 1 is answered affirmatively, for their belief?

A possible reason for overestimating how much they regard us as special is
that we know our type and it is hard to forget it. This knowledge of our type
may serve as an anchor for our beliefs – here, our second-order belief. We
may suffer from an "illusion of transparency", meaning that we may project
our knowledge about ourselves onto the other person. We may think they
know exactly how we feel.

In line with the previous chapters, however, we formulate the question by
asking for a possible underappreciation – here, one that appears in second-
order beliefs.

$$\text{Is } P^i_{P^j_{a^i}(\cdot|I^j_{\theta^i})} \text{ too close to } P^i_{P^j_{a^i}(\cdot)}?$$

Rachel fails to see that the governor has come prepared for the possibility
that she would make a plea for funding. He has interacted with many people
whose aim it is to get him to support them. Her own public profile, the
governor's personal knowledge of her, and her role during the institute visit,
are all consistent with the possibility that he may expect such a plea. Rachel
could have anticipated that he has a tested strategy to deflect it.

Conversely, the governor does not think much about how Rachel views
his personal type. He does not need to do so, anyway, since she makes no
use of her knowledge about him.

On method: how does one elicit a second-order belief?

The simple answer is that the experimenter can first elicit person j's
first-order belief and then ask person i what they think about the response
of person j to the first-order-belief question.

Clarity of the instructions is, unsurprisingly, always important. For the
procedure to be clear to the participants, person i should receive a full de-

scription of how exactly the first-order belief of person j was elicited. Ideally, person i should have the full instructions of person j available.

The measurement of second-order beliefs about ourselves considers a particular kind of meta-accuracy: we ask how well they predict us, given what they know – and how it changes if they know different things about us. A comparison of actual and believed correlations across different people can be a good measure of such second-order discrimination. Whenever different people actually view us differently, our second-order beliefs about their beliefs about us should also differ from each other, i.e., the second-order beliefs should show a non-unity correlation. If we discriminate too little, then the correlation between our (second-order) assessment on how they assess us tends to be larger than the correlation between their actual (first-order) assessments of us.

Several studies have found that people can make pretty accurate guesses about what other people think on average, but far less accurate guesses about how individual others deviate from the average. Carlson and Furr (2009) measure a respondent's assessments about how people whom they know from different contexts view them. Their questionnaire study addresses the ''main participants'' as well as several ''informants'', who are either parents or friends of the main participants. Each informant fills in a personality questionnaire about a main participant, with questions like ''On a scale from 1 to 7, can he/she easily resist temptations?''. The researchers translate these questionnaire responses into values on the Big-5 personality scales, separately by informant. The main participants fill in the same questionnaires, also separately by informant: they estimate how each informant assesses them on each question. The results show that the main participants discriminate somewhat in their second-order assessments, but not enough. For example, while they expect their parents to view them differently compared to how their friends from college view them, there is a clear under-discrimination of informants: the correlations between the two second-order assessments are far too high. Averaging across the Big-5 personality traits, the actual correlation of assements between a parent and a college friend is 0.30, whereas the main participants' meta-assessments predict that this correlation is 0.61.

Question 11: Do we underacknowledge their knowledge?

The next bit of mentalizing is about their knowledge about the state of the world. We have information about ω, and they have information about it, too. Our respective information sets are different, however, and if we do not put ourselves in their shoes and consider their view, then we may form inaccurate talking beliefs or inaccurate listening beliefs, or both.

Just like in Question 10, it is a two-step challenge. First, we need to imagine their information sets, and second, we need to imagine how they deal with each possible information set.

Our difficulty is, then, to appreciate how they use their information. Out of the countless items that are manifest to them, which ones shape their beliefs? What is the context that they focus on?

One possibility is that we may neglect that something is salient to them. We may simply not think about it and may therefore miss what they see as the point of the conversation. Another possibility is that we may expect the opposite, that they give something more attention than they actually do. Both of these effects can arise if, for instance, we simply project onto them what is salient to ourselves.

An important special case is that we may have *more* information than they. We may know something and have to lead the conversation in a way that acknowledges that they do not know it. If we do not want to give our information away, we have to be considerate about how they may learn it from the conversation. If we do want to give it away, the same is true.

Analogous arguments apply for things that are manifest to both of us but where we suspect that we pay more attention to them than they do. We can benefit from considering this asymmetry in attention and preparing our conversation accordingly. We may want to show them what things we pay attention to.

Another important case is that we may *not* know something but have to deal with the fact that they know it. Here, we have to imagine, counterfactually, each possible kind of knowledge that they could have.

All other cases of their information set being different from ours (not larger or smaller, just different), and other constellations of asymmetric attention to things that are manifest to them and us, also amount to this type of mentalizing. Depending on how carefully we imagine their information sets and how carefully we consider their beliefs for a given information set, we master our challenge of "thinking it through".

Notice a difference between first-order belief and second-order belief: the former is simpler than the latter in terms of the information conditions. The utility-relevant part of our first-order belief relates only to the information set, or circumstance, that we are actually in. There are many circumstances that we could be in, but to maximize our utility it suffices if our belief in the actual circumstance is accurate. This is different, however, for our second-order belief. There, many different information sets that the other person could be in are relevant for us. We need to consider beliefs about their belief in each one.

So, it's complicated, but we have to bite the bullet. Our best hope of making a good prediction of their belief is, indeed, to understand their possible information sets and to gauge their interpretations for each of them.

An easy special case is that a relevant piece of information is available to both interlocutors, in a way that both obviously pay attention to it. An example is the fact that Rachel and the governor are not alone in the room. This fact is important – one behaves differently in private versus in public – and it is obvious to both Rachel and the governor. It is also obvious to them that it is obvious to them, and perhaps even on higher orders of beliefs. We may call this possibility a co-presence of context.

In such a co-presence of context, there is no question about the salience of the context and we only need to assess how the other person may condition on it. However, we may still be off target in this assessment. Relevance of a context is not a black-and-white phenomenon. Recall the definition of perceived relevance, which the previous chapters introduced as a utility difference. If we fail to assess how large they perceive the utility difference to be, then we likely misperceive how they condition on the circumstance. That is, co-presence of context is a useful benchmark, but more as a qualitative idea about the coincidence of information, not so much as a quantitative property of beliefs. (And for most contextual factors, there is no co-presence anyway.)

But the idea of co-presence is a good anchor. Starting from this simple case, we can extrapolate and ask, in what ways may their information, or their beliefs, be different from ours? In what way may they not pay attention? How do they interpret what is manifest to them?

$$\text{Is } P^i_{P^j_\omega(\cdot|I^j_\omega)} \text{ too close to } P^i_{P^j_\omega(\cdot)}?$$

When judging the situation, Dimitri pays very little attention to Agniezka's beliefs. He wants something from her – that she stays on the team – and he should therefore be especially careful about her judgment of, and knowledge about, the options that the team has when going forward.

Agniezka, in fact, knows a lot. For instance, she talked to the members of the other team multiple times. Now, in the elevator, she worries about what Dimitri may know about these contacts and how he may judge her less-than-complete commitment to their own project.

A major disadvantage of laboratory research, as a method, is that one cannot be sure about external validity. This criticism applies to communication quite forcefully: humans may understand other humans better, and certainly differently, if they interact in the context-rich real world. The rather sterile laboratory environment may influence the way in which signals are used, in hard-to-predict ways. The co-presence of context may be amiss in the laboratory.

This concern may be even stronger for a study that elicits second-order beliefs. Is such an elicitation not far from real life? Do humans really think about what others think? In terms of probabilities? For each of a whole list of information sets that they may be in? All of this seems highly unlikely.

Chapter 9 will return to the issue. As a brief preview, indeed the concern is serious. It may be hard, and sometimes impossible, to elicit good proxies of the interlocutors' mentalizing about each other. But an imperfect measurement may be better than none.

Another line of defense against this criticism: laboratory studies are at least *replicable*. If one has reason to suspect that a particular feature distorts the results of a study, then one can replicate the study and leave out, or modify, the critical feature. In particular, one can modify the context. This is, of course, a variant of the main advantage of laboratory studies: control.

The researcher's imagination can be at work in a flexible playground.

Question 11 is a good example where the experimenter's control is important. Measuring how a participant views the way in which other participants use *their* information requires much transparency about what information each participant has. Experiments can provide such clarity.

Notice also that the above concern presents, in itself, an interesting set of research questions. If interlocutors indeed do not usually think through other people's information sets, then it is all the more plausible that interesting belief biases may be found.

```
The so-called hindsight bias is an example of information pro-
jection (''I knew it all along...'') in that we find it hard to
imagine that other people, when they made their decisions in the
past, did not know what we know now. With hindsight, we judge their
actions unfairly or otherwise inaccurately. Camerer et al. (1989)
show that the hindsight bias can appear in markets. One group of
experimental participants predicts the market price of an asset at
the end of 1980, being informed of all previous end-of-year prices
up to 1979. A second group was informed about the event that the
first group had to predict: in addition to being informed about
prices up to 1979, they also saw the realized price at the end of
1980. The members of the second group were then asked to predict
what the participants in the first group would predict about the
1980 price. These predictions of predictions are far too close to
the realized price. The second group cannot un-know the 1980 price
and tends to behave as if others knew it, too.
```

Question 12: Do we ignore that they judge us in context?

When predicting our actions, they factor in what they know about the world. With the same reasoning as in Question 3 we can argue that, indeed, they can predict our actions better if they discriminate between different contexts. Do we consider that they do so, to an appropriate extent?

The context helps us in this. Consciously or sub-consciously, we may "just know" what other people, in a given context, expect from us. And even if intuition cannot be trusted, the context is still prone to influence our second-order belief. The desire to fulfill what is expected from us may guide our actions – it may be a strong motivator and it may lead us to form accurate second-order beliefs.

The literature on psychological game theory investigates the role of second-order beliefs analytically: in deviation from standard game theory, it lets the payoff that an agent receives from an interaction depend directly on beliefs. For instance, if we believe that they expect us to be kind to them, then we feel guilty if we do not live up to this perceived expecation, and we obtain a lower utility because of this feeling of guilt.

The nature of second-order beliefs is thus an important part of the equilibrium in a psychological game: guilt aversion may lead to kindness. The second-order belief may, however, differ from context to context. In a new circumstance we may think that something else is expected from us – and guilt aversion may thus be irrelevant, or lead to other behaviors.

Likewise, context determines the politeness of statements. If our second-order belief is inaccurate in a particular context (i.e., we do not understand what is expected from us) then we may say something inappropriate, or perceive their statements as putting us on the spot.

(A side note: Linguists use the word *power* to describe the possibility to influence each other's actions in a conversation. Power is still another important part of context: the social relation between talker and listener determines who can steer the other's actions. Power, in turn, is not written in stone. It is surprisingly fluid, especially during a conversation.)

Summing this discussion up, we note how widely second-order beliefs set the stage for the conversation and that they, and their accuracy, depend on context. Similar to its open-ended view on first-order beliefs, the book views these possibilities, once again, as empirical questions.

Recall, finally, that the previous two questions have already indicated a pattern of failing to realize how the other person may differentiate between their information sets: we may be egocentric and project our view of the world onto them. Our information set is only one – it is not differentiated. In contrast, their information set is variable, from our perspective. We should view their expectation about us in a differentiated way, too.

$$\text{Is } P^i_{P^j_{a^i}(\cdot|I^j_\omega)} \text{ too close to } P^i_{P^j_{a^i}(\cdot)}?$$

Steve expects that Ralph views his, Steve's, part in the conversation in light of the awkward context. He expects that Ralph expects him to make a statement that refers to Ralph's miserable state of mind, which would violate their power relation by inducing Ralph to talk about something that he does not want to talk about. Steve also expects that Ralph believes that Steve will likely gossip to other schoolchildren later, telling them about the unusual encounter. All of these second-order beliefs are a misunderstanding, as Ralph did not really expect anything from Steve.

For Ralph, in turn, Steve is nothing more than a nuisance in the present situation. He does not give much thought to Steve's beliefs about his, Ralph's, actions. He thus also fails to notice that Steve is unusually afraid of a violent outburst.

A simple way of manipulating the knowledge about others' knowledge is to create co-presence of events, as described in the discussion of Question 11. In an experiment, one can easily manipulate the context in a way that both person i and person j not only know about the manipulation, but they also know that the other knows about the manipulation, and so on.

Such a manipulation should, if possible, keep everything else constant. In particular, it should keep the material incentives constant. The manipulation of context is, then, a pure *framing manipulation*.

Dufwenberg et al. (2011) have their participants play a public-good game with different frames. In their game, each of three players chooses how much of her cash endowment to allocate to a private account, and how much to a public account that is jointly owned by all three players. Both accounts are paid out at the end of the experiment. Individually, each player has an incentive to free ride on the other players and contribute nothing to the public account. But the public account receives a subsidy from the experimenter, who increases the account balance by 50 percent before the account is shared. This implies that it is collectively better for all players if each player contributes to the public account, the more the better. To measure expectations and their connection to the players' actions, the authors ask the participants to state both first-order beliefs about the contributions of the other two players, and second-order beliefs about the other two players' beliefs about their (respective) co-players' first-order beliefs. The authors also induce a framing manipulation where in one treatment the game is described as a ''giving'' game, whereas in another treatment it is described as a ''taking'' game. In a ''giving'' game, the positive-sounding frame may induce a more generous social norm -- which indeed appears. First-order beliefs are more optimistic in the ''giving'' than in the ''taking'' game, with expected contribution levels of 7.5 tokens versus 4.8 tokens, out of an available budget of 20 tokens. That is, the mere labeling affects how much the participants expect others to contribute. This also shows in their second-order beliefs, with an average of 8.1 tokens in ''giving'', versus 5.3 tokens in ''taking''. On average, second-order beliefs are fairly accurate, even in the way that they react to the labeling. The experiment also shows that while all beliefs are too optimistic, the differentiation between the two treatments' beliefs translates into actions: participants actually contribute 5.2 tokens on average in ''giving'', significantly more than the 3.8 tokens that the participants contribute in ''taking''.

Chapter 7

Perceiving how they talk

Continuing to apply the book's main trick, we now ask about our view of how they talk. That is, the questions in this chapter are analogous to those in Chapter 4 ("Talking") except that we consider them from the other side of the table. We listen, by mentalizing about their talking.

Some communication scientists regard the ability to listen to others as the most fundamental social skill of all. This is, in part, due to the observation that the success of a conversation lies not only in a mutual understanding of what is said, but also in the acknowledgement thereof. If the listener can signal to the talker that she is understood, both may feel that the conversation was worth its while.

As in other parts of this book, we focus on smaller steps, namely on listening beliefs. They are only one component of this feedback process: our understanding of what they say. We learn about the two uncertain aspects that their statement may indicate: their future actions and the state of the world.

The other person's challenge is quite different from ours. The only uncertain aspect that they try to predict, when talking, is our reaction to their statement. This chapter therefore asks about our belief about their belief about our reaction to their possible statements.

73

    https://doi.org/10.11647/OBP.0367.07

Question 13: Do we think they think we don't listen?

Earlier questions in this book focus on how our talking is explained by our first-order talking belief. Now we apply this reasoning to their talking: do we correctly predict their first-order talking belief?

Let us give this a name: our subjective expectation about their first-order talking belief is *our second-order listening belief.*

Our aim is to have an accurate version of this belief, meaning that we understand their belief with sufficient precision. This sounds doable – or not? Recall that a first-order talking belief is a rich collection of beliefs, with a separate belief for each combination of a possible statement and a possible information set that the talker could be in. Accuracy of our second-order listening belief thus asks for a lot: that we correctly predict how they predict our reaction to every possible statement, not just the one that they actually make, and that this correctness of prediction applies to each of their possible information sets.

We interpret their statement in light of this collection of beliefs. Returning to a word used earlier, this interpretation is how the statement "means" something to us.

Let us say this again, and more slowly. We have an understanding of what they expect us to do in reaction to their statement. How important this expected reaction is for them, and what they believe about the reaction, depends on their circumstance. We therefore have an understanding of the circumstances in which they would likely say what they say, and in what other circumstances they would likely not say it. Hearing their statement therefore changes our expectation about their circumstance. We learn something about their type and about the state of the world.

Notice how these arguments are intertwined with our knowledge about their incentives. What do they *want* us to do? When we interpret their statement, we consider their incentives to influence us.

The previous paragraph implies that our (first-order) beliefs about their type are an important part of our listening, too. When we assess their perceived relevance of a piece of information – and generally, when we assess their incentive to influence us – we differentiate by their possible types. In some cases, we have a pretty good idea about their type anyway. In other cases we do not, but we can analyze the situation type by type, and piece together by aggregating over the type-specific predictions. In any case, we need to consider each of their possible types separately, one at a time.

Let us first consider the case that our incentives are aligned well enough. This means that the same actions that benefit us, relative to other actions that we could choose, also benefit them. If so, then they may want us to learn something. They may believe that if we knew about a certain circumstance, we would follow our common (aligned) incentives and choose the action that is optimal in this circumstance.

They may therefore choose a message that is informative: a message that is distinctive for the circumstance that they want us to learn about.

This sounds nice and easy, but it asks for a lot of consistency between their beliefs and our beliefs. Perhaps, it asks for too much? How would they know which of their statements leads to what possible reaction from us? Do we know the extent to which they believe it? Only if their belief about our reaction coincides with our belief about their belief about our reaction do we indeed understand them. Quite a requirement! If, in contrast, the beliefs do not coincide, our understanding fails. In other words, the extent to which our second-order listening belief is accurate influences the extent to which their statement is informative to us.

What if our incentives are not aligned enough? In this case, we cannot both gain from such a coordination. They may try to induce us to choose something that is good for them – but bad for us. We, in turn, may or may not understand this. Notice how, perhaps surprisingly, this amounts to the exact same question that we discussed in the previous paragraph: our understanding of their circumstance relies on the accuracy of our second-order listening belief. This property holds even if our incentives are not aligned. And, the same reasoning also applies in all cases where our incentives are partially aligned, i.e., aligned for only some of our actions or only for some of their circumstances.

Careful: in this discussion, there does not exist a "truth" of statements. Statements can be freely associated with the circumstances in which they are uttered. What we, as the listener, understand to be the meaning of a statement is merely the connection between the statement and the circumstance in which we believe them, the talker, to make the statement.

But words like "truth" or "lies" pop up in our mind: we wonder about the correlation between statements and circumstances – and the fact that we wonder about it helps us, in particular, to understand whether they want to trick us.

Always, let us keep in mind that accuracy of our second-order listening belief is different from accuracy of our first-order listening belief. Accuracy of our second-order listening belief is about our understanding of what they believe. Accuracy of our first-order listening belief describes our expectation of their actions and the state of the world directly, by saying that this expectation conditions accurately on the statement and on our information.

The two concepts are not even nested. An accurate first-order listening belief may occur together with an inaccurate second-order listening belief – we may correctly understand the implication of a statement even if we do not understand what they think about our reaction. Likewise, an accurate second-order listening belief may occur together with an inaccurate first-order listening belief – we may understand what they expect from us in response to a statement even if we don't know what it indicates.

But the two beliefs are connected in a simple way: the inner layer is the basis of the outer layer. Our belief about their future actions and about the state of the world depends on our belief about their belief. In this sense, the second-order listening belief *causes* the first-order listening belief.

Causation is a strong claim, so let us be slower and more precise, once again. We assumed in Chapter 2 that both interlocutors not only maximize subjective expected utility, but also know this property about each other. This implies that person i's first-order belief about person j predicts a best response to person i's second-order belief: the talking strategy that person i predicts for person j maximizes person j's payoff, given person i's knowledge about this payoff and given person i's second-order belief. The first-order belief is, thus, tied to the second-order belief. May this connection – strictly speaking, a logical implication – suffice for using the word causation.

(But notice also that the second-order belief does not fully determine the first-order belief. Even with a given second-order belief, our first-order belief about the other person's type, or our a-priori belief about the state of the world, may both be more or less correct. This variability – a degree of freedom in the analysis – exists independently from second-order beliefs and it therefore enables the possibility that first-order beliefs are inaccurate despite the presence of accurate second-order beliefs, or vice versa.)

Summing all of this up, it is plausible in many conversations that an inaccuracy of second-order listening beliefs (at the inner layer) leads to an inaccuracy of first-order listening beliefs (at the outer layer): if we do not understand what they expect from us, then we likely fail to interpret well what they say.

$$\text{Is } P^i_{P^j_{a^i}(\cdot|a^j)} \text{ too close to } P^i_{P^j_{a^i}(\cdot)}?$$

While Ralph understands that Steve expects him, Ralph, to make a decision about the ball game, he misperceives Steve's first-order talking belief about what would have happened after a statement that enquires about Ralph's state of despair. Ralph therefore does not understand that Steve's question is a defensive statement that he uses to avoid incurring Ralph's wrath.

For the purpose of measurement, a big plus of asking about second-order belief accuracy – the congruence of person i' second-order belief and person j's first-order belief – is that we compare like with like (belief with belief).

Strictly speaking, the previous paragraph is utterly mistaken: the second-order belief is a probability distribution of a probability distribution of an action, which is harder to describe than a first-order belief. The latter has one "a-probability-distribution-of" less.

But we can rescue the mistaken paragraph. To make the elicitation of a second-order belief manageable for the participants in an experiment, one can ask for the means of all relevant distributions, as point beliefs. This can be done in simple words ("What do you think is their prediction about your reaction, on average?") that do not even require that the participants realize the complications of distributions over distributions. It is a quick-and-dirty solution, but one that is unlikely to distort the results.

Another practical issue is that the number of beliefs that are to be elicited is getting larger and larger. Talking beliefs include not only the (believed) reaction to the statement that the talker actually makes, but also those regarding the alternative statements that she could have made. If the talker, on top of all this, also faces separate possible circumstances (constellations of information sets) then separate second-order beliefs need to be elicited from the listener, one for each circumstance. This may require a lot of data collection.

A nice trick to reduce the amount of data is to use a stylized game where everything is mirror symmetric. That is, to use a game where symmetric constellations of the states of the world, the talker's statements, and the listener's reactions to the statements, lead to identical payoffs. In such a game, it suffices to measure fewer beliefs and make inferences about the "mirrored" constellations.

Grabova et al. (2023) conduct a constant-sum game where the talker knows the state of the world, which could be A or B. The listener only knows that the two states are equally likely to occur. The talker's two possible messages are also labeled ''A'' and ''B'' and she sends one of these messages at will. Messages have no direct payoff consequences but the listener chooses one of two payoff-relevant actions, which are also called ''A'' or ''B''. The symmetry is completed by allowing only two payoffs in this game, such that one player is the winner and earns the high payoff, whereas the other loses and receives the low payoff. The identity of winner and loser is state-action dependent: in each state, the listener wins if his action matches the state and the talker wins if the listener's action does not match the state. The game thereby induces a very transparent incentive for the talker to try and mislead the listener about the true state of the world. Since the game is symmetric regarding the labels ''A'' and ''B'', the entire data collection can be done under the scenario that one particular message, ''A'', is been sent, and all answers can be applied also to the other possible message. That is, the sender is only asked: ''Suppose that you sent the message 'A'. How likely do you think it is the receiver chooses 'A'?'' For second-order beliefs, the listener is asked to predict the talker's answer to this question. All beliefs about states/messages with ''B'' can be inferred from this, under the reasonable assumption that the participants have beliefs that do not depend on the label. In effect, the experiment provides a simple set of measures for first-order and second-order beliefs about truth telling and trust. The results show that second-order listening beliefs are fairly accurate on average: the average predictions of the listener's probability

of trusting the message is close to one half, in both the talker's
first-order talking belief and the listener's second-order listening belief. One half is also the equilibrium prediction -- a
babbling equilibrium. A data pattern that contradicts game theory
is, however, that the heterogeneity in listeners' second-order
beliefs moves in the wrong direction: listeners who believe that
the talker expects them to trust the message do indeed trust the
message with higher likelihood. This is inconsistent with the incentives in the game because a talker who first-order believes that
the listener trusts his message is more likely, not less likely,
to lie. (This is theoretically and empirically true.) A listener
who has such a second-order belief should therefore be less, not
more, trusting. The data thus indicate a limitation of asking for
second-order listening beliefs: at least for some of the experimental participants, the reported beliefs apear to be poor proxies
for the participants' second-order beliefs. An alternative explanation -- one that the book's next question will pick up and that is
even less consistent with the theory -- is that these participants
do not base their decisions on second-order beliefs at all.

Question 14: Do we think they talk to us as strangers?

Our type is always with us; it is near impossible to forget. Can we nevertheless take the talker's perspective, with limited knowledge about ourselves,
while listening to them? Otherwise, we may take things personally when
they are not.

Notice how this can also have a warm, positive ring to it: we may *like*
them talking to us in a personal way.

One such possibility are white lies, i.e., deceptions that are for our, the
listener's, benefit. Many white lies are about our own type: they flatter us.
We enjoy hearing them.

Do we also believe them? Not in the sense of learning about us. We have
superior knowledge about our type. This book even takes the extreme, simplifying view that we have perfect knowledge of our type. But we do learn
about their belief about our type. The white lie may indicate that they have

a positive view of us. We may not have been sure of this before, and enjoy the update.

Is it justified, though? Under what conditions may we believe a white lie? To find an answer, recall the nature of the second-order listening belief: our belief about their belief about our reaction. Recall also that our second-order listening belief is a wide collection: it specifies what we expect them to expect from us for every possible statement that they may make and for every possible information that they may have about us. If we update from the white lie, then we must believe that there is a connection between our reaction and their circumstance, in their minds: the way in which they expect us to react must co-vary with their belief about our type. Upon hearing their statement, we can thus infer something about how they view us.

For concreteness, let us suppose that a stylized information structure governs all beliefs. We know our type and they, the talker, could be in two possible information sets: one that indicates to them that we are "for them" (i.e., that our incentives are aligned with theirs) and one that indicates to them that we are "against them" (...not aligned with theirs). Our second-order listening belief specifies what we expect them to expect us to do in each case.

Let us also consider the case that we believe that they, in both information sets, believe us to show a positive reaction – one that increases their utility – to the particular statement that we call a white lie, and a less positive reaction to not telling it. This would be a natural belief for us to have, given that the white lie flatters us.

But this second-order listening belief is not suitable to justify our credulity: since we believe them to best respond to their first-order beliefs, we must believe that they tell the white lie in both of their information sets. In each of them, they expect a positive reaction from us, so their incentives do not change across the two sets. Hearing them tell the white lie is therefore not informative for us.

That is, we cannot believe the white lie, in this case. A second-order listening belief of the above-described kind is too simple. We need to find a more involved justification. What other second-order belief would do the job?

Well, involved or not, the belief would have to be somewhat peculiar. It would need to prescribe that their belief about our reaction differs between the two information sets – although by assumption, we *cannot* differentiate between the information sets (otherwise we would not need to learn).

Likely, such a peculiar second-order listening belief would be inaccurate: it is plausible that their actual first-order talking belief does not differentiate much between their information sets. If so, then we have a misunderstanding – a mismatch between our second-order beliefs and their first-order beliefs.

The accuracy is, of course, an empirical question. It may well be that their first-order talking belief *does* differentiate between their information sets, at least to some extent. Also, recall that this is all a stylized example with a particular information strucuture. Other situations may make different predictions.

Yet, the stylized example makes a general point: thinking through the logic of white lies makes them less believable. We should realize that they have an incentive to tell the lie, and that we should not update too much because their incentive to tell the white lie may not change much with the information that they have. It is therefore hard to justify our credulity with plausible second-order listening beliefs. Rather, they may be off target, or we may disregard them altogether.

Importantly, the same reasoning often applies to "black" lies, i.e., those that do not benefit us if we believe them. Here, too, we should consider their beliefs about our reaction. Here, too, we may fail to notice that these beliefs may not depend much on their information. The talker often has, very simply, an incentive to lie to us. We often have, very simply, no way of detecting the lie.

Lie detection has other interesting aspects, too. We may believe that they do not like to lie. That is, we may attribute a preference type to them that gives them a low utility if the statement is misleading (or uninformative) about their beliefs. We think of them as being truth tellers.

This rather optimistic view is perhaps a more plausible description of our view of them, but it does not describe second-order listening beliefs. The belief that they are truth tellers is a belief about their direct utility from making a certain statement in a certain circumstance. This belief does not rely on their beliefs about our reaction.

We can summarize the discussion by saying that it is plausible that we believe a lie – nothing keeps our first-order listening beliefs from prescribing that we update – but if this credulity stems from our second-order listening belief, then it may well be inaccurate, i.e., we plausibly mispredict the other person' first-order talking belief.

$$\text{Is } P^i_{P^j_{a^i}(\cdot|a^j, I^j_{\theta i})} \text{ too close to } P^i_{P^j_{a^i}(\cdot|a^j)}?$$

Agniezka hates aggression and feels vulnerable when the gloves come off. Dimitri has observed ample evidence of her sensitivity in the past, and is aware of it. He does not, however, expect Agniezka to judge their collaboration based on the aggressiveness of his tone. Agniezka, in contrast, wonders how aware Dimitri is of her sensitivity. She expects that if Dimitri was aware of it, he would have considered his aggressive battle speech to prevent her from staying on the team. Based on this second-order listening belief, Agniezka interprets Dimitri's talking about "blood" as revealing his unawareness of her sensitivity, which makes the possibility of staying on the team even less attractive to her.

Lying and lie detection are tightly connected to the two interlocutors' second-guessing of each others' types. Misunderstandings about preferences can induce misunderstandings about the credibility of an utterance and make it to be perceived as a lie. All this is not only a qualitative discussion (lie or not; white lie or black lie): misunderstandings about preferences also determine the size of the harm, or the size of the benefit, that a lie causes. Dishonesty and distrust may be more or less hurtful, and the pursuit of a perceived mutual goal may make us feel more or less good.

Measuring this in a laboratory experiment is difficult. Many of the larger effects of a lie are emotional. One cannot install a non-trivial knowledge structure about the participants' emotional types, and one cannot even induce emotions sufficiently well. The experiments are simply too small.

Psychologists have developed a technique that nevertheless succeeds in detecting the interlocutors' emotions about each other's actions: perspective taking. All participants receive the same description of a realistic but hypothetical situation. This situation can describe any interaction of two people, including an emotionally loaded interaction. Half of the participants are asked to write a text about the situation, written in first person singular from the angle of one person in the described situation. The other half of participants do the same, but from the other person's perspective.

After the participants have taken their perspectives in this way, the experimenters can ask them about views, beliefs, preferences, etc., and measure the extent to which all of these vary between the two groups.

It is reasonable to assume that real-life differences in perspectives are more extreme than what one may find in such an experiment. After all, the participants are not really part of the described situation. Any effect of perspective taking is therefore likely to be a lower-bound estimate of the effect in a naturally occuring situation of the same kind.

Gordon and Miller (2000) describe to their participants a situation of a couple who are together for about a year. One partner, the ''lie receiver'', observes that his/her loved one -- the other partner, or ''lie teller'' -- has a restaurant lunch with a former boyfriend/girlfriend. The lie teller had not told the lie receiver about the lunch beforehand and does not even admit to it later, when asked explicitly how he/she had spent the lunch hour. The lie receiver reacts negatively and, so the story goes, the relationship's continuation is now in danger. The partipants in the experiment all read the same text, creating the same knowledge about the facts of events, including the lies that were told. They are randomly assigned to take the perspective of the lie teller or the lie receiver. (These labels are not used in the experiment -- all individuals in the story have names.) A questionnaire then elicits the participants' views about the two partners' actions, in 14 questionnaire items. Via a factor analysis, the 14 items are projected on four main factors, three of which describe whether the actions were justified, misunderstood, and common. A regression analysis shows that being randomly assigned to the perspective of the lie receiver creates the view that the lie was significantly less justified, less misunderstood, and more common, compared to the case that one is randomly assigned to take the perspective of the lie teller. The experiment thus illustrates how the judgements of the appropriateness of statements can vary between the talker and the listener even if they have identical information about the facts of a situation. In this story, the lie teller is unlikely to realize the psychic damage that the lie does and the lie receiver is unlikely to be aware of this. However, the analysis refers to a comparison of first-order beliefs and second-order beliefs only

```
somewhat vaguely and indirectly, by comparing the perceptions of
how much the lie is viewed as justified, misunderstood, and com-
mon.
```

Question 15: Do we think they predict our reaction independent of context?

Context adds a vast richness to language, which makes listening hard: much harder than deciphering a code or following a convention. No code or convention is rich enough to cover all possible meanings that arise through combinations of utterances and contexts. Understanding means interpreting their statement in light of the context.

Our second-order listening belief is suitable to capture this – because it is rich, too. They, the talker, consider the context in their first-order talking belief; our belief about their first-order talking belief allows us to consider exactly this fact. We interpret their statement by guessing how they expect us to react, depending on the circumstances that they may find themselves in.

The richness of their context-dependent talking implies, however, that our listening is ambiguous. There are too many dimensions of context that we may or may not consider in our beliefs about their beliefs. (Ambiguity may not be a bad thing. Poetry's meaning is up for grabs but this does not make poetry less valuable – quite the opposite.)

In any case, listening is more valuable if our second-order belief considers context well, i.e., if we realize what dimension of the state of the world their first-order talking belief conditions on. How do we identify this dimension?

To answer this, it is useful to recall Chapter 4's discussion of perceived relevance. As talker, we choose our statement because we anticipate that in light of a particular context, the statement generates a response from them that enhances our utility. Now, as listener, we understand that their first-order belief is analogous. They choose their statement because they anticipate, in light of a particular circumstance, a utility-enhancing response from us. They perceive some piece of the context as relevant. We listen well if our second-order listening belief reacts to this piece, too.

In this search for context, it helps that we already know their statement.

We know that they, as talker, choose this statement to generate the best possible outcome for themselves. We examine our belief about their belief to assess why they regard this statement as optimal.

This reasoning helps us to reduce the ambiguity. They could have said so many other things – the opportunity cost of talking. We can assess this opportunity cost: our second-order listening belief indicates the extent to which they believe that each of the alternative statements would have generated an alternative benefit. Our second-order listening belief thereby justifies their choice of the particular statement that they make, and it reduces the set of candidate contexts along the way: the talker must perceive their statement to yield a higher benefit than each of the alternative statements, and the context that they condition on must contribute to this perception.

Paraphrasing this in simpler words: We may know what they are talking about because our second-order belief, in connection with the statement that we hear, indicates what context is perceived relevant for them.

Or, we may fail to know it. As always in this book, it is an empirical question.

$$\text{Is } P^i_{P^j_{a^i}(\cdot|a^j, I^j_\omega)} \text{ too close to } P^i_{P^j_{a^i}(\cdot|a^j)} ?$$

The governor does not take the issue of stolen artifacts very seriously. His second-order listening belief fails to examine a particular dimension of context: Rachel and he already have a previous thread of conversation, namely the once-started initiative on cultural policies. Normally, it would be in Rachel's interest to talk about this topic. (She could ask him to fund it, too.) Nevertheless, she decides to talk about the stolen artifacts, which signals her sense of urgency for this new topic. It is likely that she has reasons to regard it as more relevant than the old one.

Context variation can provide a benchmark for comparison. "To put something in context" often means that we compare the size, or importance, of an item with another item that the context provides. In a laboratory study, the experimenter can measure the reaction to a stimulus in the presence or absence of such a quantitative context.

This simple trick can also be used in experimental studies of language evolution. A sizable set of research pursues this approach, some of them by studying non-human animals or children.

Barner and Snedeker (2008) provide an example that demonstrates how 4-year-old children's understanding of words reacts to context information. The authors run an experiment that investigates how the children connect the context-dependent adjective ''tall'' with a novel set of objects that come under the made-up name ''pimwit''. When is a pimwit tall? The task of a participating child is to examine 9 such novel objects, the pimwits, and classify each of them as tall or short. (To connect this situation to our discussion, we view the child as the listener and we view the experimenter as the talker who says: ''Point at pimwits that are tall.'' The child's reaction reflects his or her second-order belief about what the experimenter expects him or her to do.) In the experiment, pimwits are little figures of varying height between 1 and 9 inches, with a one inch difference in height among each pair of adjacent pimwits. The average pimwit has, thus, a height of 5 inches. To create context, a second group of four distractor objects is placed alongside the nine target pimwits. These distractor object are of a similar physical style as the pimwits but they are not labelled at all and the children are not asked to evaluate them. Instead, the distractor objects only sit on the table, acting as a potential reference set for the nine target pimwits. In the SHORT DISTRACTOR treatment, the distractor objects have an average height of only 1.25 inches, whereas in the TALL DISTRACTOR treatment, the distractors' average height is 8.75 inches. Indeed, the children classify many more of the nine target pimwits as ''tall'' in SHORT DISTRACTOR than in TALL DISTRACTOR: the average heights of the marginal (smallest) pimwits that are classified as tall in the two treatments are 5.4 and 8.4 for SHORT DISTRACTOR and TALL DISTRACTOR, respectively. The experiment thus shows that even at this early age, the interpretation of language is context dependent. (Or especially at this age?) A further variation shows that the children also use the precise specification of the context: in a variant of SHORT DISTRACTOR, the distractor objects are endowed with their own name, ''tulvets'', and are painted in a different color from that of the target pimwits but have the same heights as the distractor objects in SHORT DISTRACTOR. In this condition the marginal height of the pimwits that the children classify as tall is significantly higher, at 6.9 inches. This result is similar to another experiment where no distractor objects are

shown at all, yielding an average height of the marginal ''tall''
pimwit of 7.2 inches. That is, the 4-year olds appear to use the
distractor objects as a comparison set only if their specification
suggests to do so. Overall, the children show remarkable reactions
to context in their second-order beliefs. The experiment cannot
give evidence, however, on whether these second-order beliefs are
accurate, as it does not measure the talker's first-order talking
belief.

Chapter 8

Perceiving how they listen

Recall from Chapter 4 that we anticipate how they may react to each of our statements – as described by our first-order talking belief. We now aim to support this belief, by turning the table on Chapter 5 and asking how we perceive their listening belief: how we understand their belief change upon hearing the statement. This belief change translates into a reaction, i.e., what we care about.

(A nasty note of caution over two paragraphs, which the reader may want to ignore: let us always keep track of who has what information. When considering how they listen, we condition on their possible information sets. There are many of them, and we have to consider them all. All of *our* beliefs depend on our own information. In particular, our beliefs about their beliefs also depend on our own information.

Nevertheless, we do not need to re-consider each of their circumstances separately for each of our possible circumstances. It suffices to discuss the questions that arise in this chapter simply for one of our possible circumstances, namely the one that we are in. This shortcut stems from the fact that this chapter only asks about the inner layer. It considers what we believe about how they update their listening beliefs; these updates depend only on their, the other person's, information sets, not on ours.)

 https://doi.org/10.11647/OBP.0367.08

Question 16: Do we think they just don't listen?

They hear our statement and react to it. Our (outer-layer) expectation of this reaction is our first-order talking belief and underpins our talking. We now justify the first-order talking belief, and hence our talking, through a perceived first-order listening belief.

To see how exactly this belief underpins our talking, we proceed with the usual slowness. First, a name. Our subjective expectation about their first-order listening belief is called, no surprise, *our second-order talking belief.* It is accurate if it correctly predicts their first-order listening belief for each possible statement and each information set that they could be in.

With an accurate second-order talking belief, we correctly understand how they would update from each of our statements, in each possible circumstance of theirs. Realistically, we cannot achieve exact accuracy – but we should try. The more accurate our second-order talking belief is, the better we predict what their reaction to each statement is, and the better is our choice of statement. A more accurate second-order talking belief increases our utility.

The correct use of their information is a challenge and makes this question interesting. Just like we use our information when listening – see Chapter 5 – we consider how they use theirs. We imagine how they consider their information about our type and how they consider their information about the context. This results in a quite rich interplay between second-order beliefs and first-order beliefs, in a similar way to that in Chapter 7. Just like we did there, we can ask the questions about meaning (Question 13), about lies (14) and about the richness of language (15).

Indeed, many things are the same from both sides. For another example, recall the importance of aligned interest in Chapter 7, which is equally important here. Whether or not the incentives are aligned influences whether we can both gain from the statement, versus only one of us. Second-order beliefs reflect this, and they thus reflect how much information we, as talker, believe to transmit. Still another analogy to Chapter 7 is that an accurate second-order talking belief does not imply that the first-order talking belief is accurate; and vice versa.

But there are differences, too. In this chapter, *we* are the talker and our statement carries meaning to *them*. We know the connection between our circumstances and our statement because we choose the statement ourselves. They, as listener, need to figure it out. The fact that we already know the connection may help our second-order belief's accuracy, or reduce it. Another difference – one that helps *their* belief – is that they hear the statement that we make and can condition their beliefs on the fact that we make it. We, as talker, have to consider different statements without the additional information that one of them is chosen. For all these reasons, second-order talking beliefs require a different kind of mentalizing than second-order listening beliefs. It may be that when we listen, we have accurate second-order beliefs but when we talk, we fail to have them – or the other way around.

Notice, finally, that in many conversations we talk because we may *want* to change their expectations, for reasons of vanity. We may love to surprise. (It may be the reason why we are in the conversation in the first place.) In other conversations, we may want to keep a secret from them.

At the core of all these cases lies our second-order belief accuracy. How well do we assess the extent to which our statements changes their belief?

$$\text{Is } P^i_{P^j_x(\cdot|a^i)} \text{ too close to } P^i_{P^j_x(\cdot)}?$$

Here, and also in Questions 17 and 18, we let $x \in \{\omega, \tilde{a}^i\}$, in analogy to the description in Question 7.

Dimitri, ill-prepared for the elevator conversation, does not anticipate that Agniezka understands his statement as indicating that he would not blame her if she left the project now. Furthermore, he does not anticipate that describing his vision of the team's possible joint future makes Agniezka's belief about this joint future only more gloomy. In his current state of mind, everything that he talks about would sound negative to her. It may have been more effective for Dimitri to talk about the possibility of the team splitting up.

The illusion of transparency is a direct obstacle to the accuracy of second-order talking beliefs: we tend to overestimate how well they know our circumstance. We may therefore, erroneously, think that we need not describe it.

Conversely, in a situation where we want to hide our circumstance, we may underestimate how well we can do it. We are better liars than we think.

For an experimental demonstration of the illusion of transparency, one need not specify the set of possible statements with much detail. It suffices to measure first-order listening beliefs about the truth status of a statement (whatever the statement is) and compare it with the talker's second-order talking belief.

```
Gilovich et al. (1998) provide a nice demonstration of the il-
lusion of transparency: one group of participants, the ''drinkers'',
participate one by one and are asked to drink five drinks of equal
visual appearance while being watched by a second group of par-
ticpants, the ''observers''. One of the five drinks has a foul
taste but the drinkers are asked not to show which one it is. An
observer's task is to watch the drinker drink and to identify,
from their demeanor, the foul-tasting drink. That is, he or she
attempts to detect a lie: the instance of the drinking excercise
where the drinker only pretends not to be disgusted. After drink-
ing, the drinkers report their second-order beliefs: they predict
how many of the observers have correctly identified their feeling
of disgust. The actual detection rate is 20%, so the observers are
no more accurate than guessing randomly. But the drinkers predict
that a significantly larger share of the observers, 36%, identify
the true circumstance.
```

Question 17: Do we think they interpret our statements and other people's statements in the same way?

We usually do not say as much as we could say. Our language is vague and does not specify all the detail. As discussed for Question 15, the rich variety of contexts makes it even less conceivable that we specify all the detail. Yet, vagueness sometimes increases eloquence and can help to make ourselves clear.

Importantly, a statement's effect on the listener is not only a matter of the words that we use: how we believe to influence the listener depends a lot on what we know about them, and what they know about us. For certain constellations of types, it may well be that using vague language is our best option.

A well-known game-theoretic analogue of this is the impossibility of informative equilibria in the presence of conflicting interests. If our and their incentives are not well aligned, an equilibrium where we speak in a fully informative way is ruled out by a simple contradiction argument. Suppose that we could talk to them in such a fully informative equilibrium. Then we would attempt to influence them and move their belief away from the truth, at least a little bit, in the direction that helps us the most. This deviation would not help them, by the assumption of conflicting interests. They know this and would therefore not listen to everything that we say. The equilibrium therefore cannot be fully informative.

An equilibrium with vague language, in contrast, can well exist if the incentives are not too disaligned. For instance, we are able to indicate to them a rough summary of our information – whether it falls into one rough category, or another. They cannot infer anything precise from such a vague indication, but at least they learn the rough summary. Note the equilibrium property: Given how they listen, we actually want to make such a vague indication because it is the best we can do. And they, in turn, have no reason to fear that we trick them, given that our language is vague and does not allow micro-managed influences of their reaction.

The reasoning is an equilibrium argument and it therefore involves higher-order beliefs. But of course it also involves beliefs of lower order. So let us consider to what extent we can tell the same story while restricting ourselves to first-order beliefs and second-order beliefs.

To tell the story, we compare the value of a vague statement with that of a precise one. The hypothesis that the vague statement is optimal, expressed as a property of our second-order talking belief, is that we expect that they update weakly more (in a direction that helps us) in response to the vague statement than in response to the precise one.

Why would we expect this? The precise information has all the information of the vague statement, and more.

It is, however, certainly a feasible belief. We may expect them to learn the wrong thing if we give them too much information, i.e., that it misleads them or keeps them from listening to the key part of what we say.

A deeper reason has to do with our type. A long and elaborate statement may change their view of our preferences. It may emphasize our type and our hope for a particular, fine-tuned reaction. That is, a more detailed statement may make them suspicious.

This reasoning goes back to asking about what is (perceived) relevant. Talking has a cost, so if we talk with much detail, we must believe that there is a benefit in doing so. Our expectation must be that they respond positively to the detailed talking. But this expectation requires that we have a detailed view of their type, to the extent that they share our interest even about our detailed utterances. We must regard the details as relevant, and believe that they are relevant for the listener, too. This directs attention to the question of preference alignment: if their preferences are not so congruent with ours, then this fact, too, becomes more salient. They may ask themselves how much they share, or trust, our preference.

A more general observation is that we use *ostension* when we talk. We point to something. We use the fact that the listener knows about our opportunity cost: we could do something else with our time and energy – e.g., say something different. Given this opportunity cost, the fact that we say something specific makes it obvious to the listener that we expect a reaction to this specific statement. This, in turn, sends the listeners on a search for a motivation for the specific statement, i.e., for a context that we perceive as relevant if it is combined with the statement.

Question 18 and Chapter 9 will return to the issue of context for the listener. Anticipating this discussion, we notice that our doubts about our ability for precise language, as expressed in the previous paragraphs, may become even stronger if we try to justify our second-order talking belief by introducing more levels: beliefs of third and higher order. The more we ask about what we believe about each other's type and the beliefs about these beliefs, the more questionable it may appear that our preferences are well-enough aligned to convey much information.

A more language-oriented view of vagueness generates further possible effects. Linguists, psychologists and philosophers have examined that vagueness is far more than just imprecision. A statement that is merely imprecise can conceivably be made more precise, for instance by using a longer and more detailed sentence. But many vague statements cannot even conceivably be subject to such a "precification". (Think of poetry again.) Instead, they are simply a different category of statement. They may therefore evoke a belief change that is different from anything that a precise statement can evoke.

Even these linguistic aspects of second-order talking beliefs are connected with what they think about our type. We may believe that they, when hearing a vague statement, may think of us as being friendly or wise, or perhaps as useless or offensive. Their interpretation of our statement depends on how they view us and our second-order belief about it, correspondingly, contains large degrees of freedom.

$$\text{Is } P^i_{P^j_x(\cdot|a^i,I^j_{\theta i})} \text{ too close to } P^i_{P^j_x(\cdot|a^i)}?$$

Rachel is a scientist who uses fairly precise language. Her statement about having "verified the reports with scientific studies" is not exaggerated. She knows about the reliability of her statement, and she does not like to simplify or boast. Her second-order talking belief specifies that the governor understands her type in this respect. She therefore expects that he understands her words to be literally true (give and take). The governor does not, however, view her type in this way – he does not regard Rachel as an authority for truth, any more than most other people with whom he interacts – and he therefore does not entertain the possibility that her statements describe a significant political risk for him.

Being personally close with the person to whom we talk may make our second-order talking beliefs more accurate. But they may also become less accurate if we know the listener well.

Experimenters can make the appropriate measurement for this question by simply combining measures that were previously discussed in the book. The experimenter can vary the identity of the listener and measure how the second-order listening beliefs varies with it, relative to how the different listeners' first-order listening beliefs change. To demonstrate that the listener's identity creates a bias, it suffices to carry out the exercise for a given statement, or a small set of statements.

A surprising pattern of results in psychology shows the extent of misunderstandings among spouses. Savitzky et al. (2011) conduct a communication experiment where they record the expectation of participants on how well they expect to be understood.

The talkers say a pre-determined phrase that has multiple possible
meanings, like ``What a nice pen'', which could indicate that one
is about to grab the pen, or that one would like to know who owns
it. Four different interpretations are listed on the experimental
instructions, for each statement. The talker is under instruction
to convey one of the interpretations via their way of uttering the
phrase, using variations in their speaking tone in any way they
like. The listeners then indicate one of the four candidate interpretations. Before the listeners' interpretations are revealed,
the talkers are asked to predict in how many of ten phrases they
expect the listeners to grasp the intended meaning. The experiment, crucially, also varies the identity of the listener. When
talking to a stranger, talkers predict that a little more than
five phrases are understood in the intended way, whereas in truth
a little less than four were understood. When talking to one's
spouse, the actual understanding was almost at the same level -
roughly four phrases were interpreted in the intended way - but
talkers believed that more than six phrases were identified correctly. The results indicate an over-conditioning of second-order
talking beliefs, for the case that one's spouse is the listener.

Question 18: Do we fail to see how their inter-pretations are in context?

Choosing the topic of our statement, we play with the difference between
what is merely manifest to our listener, on the one hand, and what they
believe to be relevant, on the other hand. We make references to certain dimensions of the state of the world, influencing what is salient to them. Their,
the listener's, information about the world – all things that are manifest to
them – is more than what they can process. We re-direct their focus and we
do this better if we understand how their first-order listening belief reacts to
context.

Given the high dimensionality of context, it is quite a miracle that they
understand us at all. Yes, we can influence their focus, but how far does this
take us? There are so many dimensions of context and, with them, there are
so many possibilities of interpretating our statements. But it works, at least
somewhat. The human mind's strive towards efficiency has lead to great
mastery of language. Talking and listening are highly efficient ways of pro-

cessing information. In a haystack of possible meanings, we and they both have a good idea of where to search for the needle.

This efficient selection of the contexts has, once again, a lot to do with relevance and utility maximization. As discussed for Question 17, we use ostension when we talk, i.e., we point to things. They know that we choose the statement in a way that is best for us. The fact that we point to something means that we expect them to react to this fact – otherwise our ostension would be a waste of time and effort.

A short way of putting it: utility is benefit minus cost and for a context to be relevant for us when we talk, it must therefore be (i) accessible to them (low cost of connecting our statement with it), (ii) accessible to us (ditto), (iii) beneficial to us (their reaction helps us) and (iv) perceived beneficial to them (they believe it helps them). This narrows down the interpretation.

Our second-order talking belief reflects this reasoning. If we believe that their first-order listening belief makes a particular context perceived relevant for them, then we believe that their reaction depends on this context. We, too, can condition our statement on the context and, between the two of us, we can transport meaning more successfully by conditioning on the same context.

That is, the relevance of contexts are likely to be connected between the two interlocutors, at least in our mind. Clearly, our beliefs may be wrong. We will surely not be able to anticipate perfectly how each context is relevant for them, but the closer a fit we obtain, the better it is for us.

Notice again the asymmetry between their role and ours. They, as listener, cannot influence our belief about the relevant context – only we can influence theirs, through our statement. The listener's perceived relevance of a particular context may change with the statement they hear. The ability to influence the perceived relevance of context is, in all this, the talker's alone.

One way of justifying our second-order belief is to link it to a third-order belief: we believe that they condition on a certain context because we think about their second-order listening belief. If we have a reasonable belief about how they respond to their belief about our belief, then we may be more confident in our own second-order belief. In principle, one can carry this further, to justify the third-order belief by fourth-order beliefs, and so on.

But for many considerations, this type of deeper thinking is not necessary: the analysis described before the previous paragraph applies even if we just take our second-order talking belief as the primitive concept. The second-order talking belief describes to what extent we perceive a context as relevant to them. This is all that we need to select our statement. And, in all this, the more accurate is the second-order belief, the smaller is our misprediction about their reaction.

$$\text{Is } P^i_{P^j_x(\cdot|a^i,I^j_\omega)} \text{ too close to } P^i_{P^j_x(\cdot|a^i)}?$$

Steve's second-order talking belief is off target, by conditioning too much on the context of Ralph's despair. In particular, Steve believes that Ralph believes that with a relatively high probability, Steve will tell other children about what he saw. Steve's statement aims to minimize this probability in Ralph's belief, i.e., it aims to express the smallest possible challenge to Ralph's authority.

Unbeknownst to Steve, the inaccuracy of his second-order talking belief is beneficial – a lucky coincidence. Steve's statement appears to be so unrelated to the context that Ralph does not connect them in his mind. Had Ralph made such a connection, he would have been more pessimistic about Steve's future actions and would have reacted more aggressively.

Experimental design is often guided by the solution of a reference theory, such as the set of Nash equilibria in a game. It is good science to determine precisely what the reference theory predicts for an experiment before actually running it.

The more general the theory is – the weaker the assumptions that it rests on – the better. The strongest experiments often have a clear prediction that is valid for a wide set of assumptions. An unambiguous theoretical prediction gives the experimenter a firm control over the interpretation of the data.

By the same token, the experimenters should stay in control of their theoretical prediction when varying the state of the world in an experiment. In cases where the variation of ω is a pure framing variation, this is usually not a problem since the theoretical prediction mostly does not react to framing.

In cases where material incentives are affected by a change in ω, retaining a clear theoretical prediction may be a challenge. But it may be surmountable – e.g., it may be possible to keep the theoretical prediction constant across different values of ω.

In an economic experiment by Agranov et al. (2023), competition is switched on and off between two treatments. In each treatment, there is a single buyer who wants to buy a good only if it is of high quality. In one treatment, NO COMPETITION, there is only one seller who observes the quality and sends a message to the buyer -- ''high quality'' or ''low quality''. As usual in buyer-seller games, the seller may have an incentive to lie to the buyer if the true quality is low. Whether or not he has this incentive depends on the credulity of the buyer. In this experiment, the seller may also incur a payoff reduction that reflects guilt aversion and/or lying aversion, and the buyer may incur a disappointment cost if she believes a lie. These possible psychological effects are private information, making the behavior of other players hard to predict. Agranov et al. (2023) formulate a precise parametric theory of these effects, in order to factor them into the analysis and predict how they differ between different contexts. In particular, competition may matter: a second treatment, COMPETITION, introduces another seller who also has a product for sale and can also send a message to the buyer. The buyer then selects a seller and, potentially, decides to buy from the selected seller. In this treatment, lies and disappointment may be evaluated very differently than in the absence of competition. Despite the relatively high complexity of the games played in this experiment, the two treatments have analogous sets of equilibria and the design allows a ceteris-paribus investigation: does competitive pressure induce more lying, and is lying more or less successful under competitive pressure? The results on the buyer's first-order listening belief show that buyers tend to believe a message that promises high quality in both treatments: the average posterior beliefs in high quality after hearing the message ''high quality'' are higher than after hearing the message ''low quality'', by a difference of 50 and 55 percentage points, in NO COMPETITION and COMPETITION, respectively. The sellers' second-order talking belief show corresponding differences of 53 and 45 percentage points in the two treatments, respectively. That is, if anything, the buyers are mildly more credulous in the treatment where the sellers face competition. The sellers, in contrast, believe that the buyers become slightly less creduluous in this treatment. But the sellers still

believe that the lie is effective, even under competition -- where
they are more likely to need it. This is consistent with the observed messages by sellers. They lie more than twice as often in
COMPETITION than in NO COMPETITION.

Chapter 9

In higher order: Seeing their view of our view

In closing, we ponder more about beliefs about beliefs about beliefs.

This could go on for many more steps – one could ask infinitely many questions about higher-order beliefs in conversations. But the book is already done, as the list of 18 questions goes up only to the second order. The exception is that in the previous chapter, third-order beliefs are briefly described as a possible justification for second-order beliefs.

Why not go deeper? Emphasizing the significance of the brief "exception" in the previous chapter, one may observe that there are plenty of misunderstandings that may arise due to third-order beliefs. One example is Steve's belief that Ralph may believe that Steve views the context as relevant. For another example, consider a simple distortion of our second-order talking beliefs of Question 16: we may think that their first-order listening belief does not discriminate with respect to our statements. One possible reason for this – in third order – is that we think that they think that our first-order talking belief does not discriminate with respect to our statements either. That is, we may think that they think it is useless to listen – because they think that we think that they would not listen. If we indeed think about them in this way, then we are obviously unaware of the possible sophistication of their listening. If, in fact, their listening is sophisticated, then we miscommunicate. We may say too little. And the story continues. One can ask meaningful questions about fourth-order beliefs, and so on.

But the book stops early and this chapter merely discusses some conceptual reasons for doing so. One reason for stopping early is that it does no

    https://doi.org/10.11647/OBP.0367.09

harm: we do not miss anything that higher-order beliefs may be relevant for. Their effect on behavior, whatever this effect is, would have to pass through the lower-order beliefs. Whatever happens at the innermore layers (the higher orders) of a belief system, it is either irrelevant or it has to show at the outermore layers.

A counterargument is that the very basis of communication lies in its coordination of beliefs. That the strength of a convention and of a common understanding of context lies exactly in the higher-order beliefs. That the relevance of an utterance becomes clear only because the interlocutors know that they understand each other, know that they know it, and so on.

This counterargument is a good one, based on a large literature. Nevertheless, one can disagree with it. This book is quite precise about what can be described with second-order beliefs but without using third-order beliefs. It is a lot, as Chapters 7 and 8 have shown. References to third-order beliefs are possibly useful, but it is not necessary to make them if one wants to talk about meaning, relevance, lies, or politeness.

The following paragraphs re-examine the question of third-order beliefs with respect to the word "meaning". They will illustrate that a substantial part of an utterance's meaning shows up even if we avoid all beliefs of higher order.

So let us consider "meaning" and its connection to higher-order beliefs, as it is often done in the philosophy of language. More precisely, let us consider the following sentence: "By saying statement a^i to person j, person i means p." Here, p is any given proposition (i.e., a possible truth, perhaps about the state of the world) and we will interpret the expression "means p" as saying that person i believes that the statement induces a change in person j's belief that is consistent with this proposition p.

How does statement a^i achieve this? A helpful discussion from the literature is the view that i expects to successfully communicate p by saying something that she believes will make j realize her, i's, *intention* to communicate p.

The logic is compelling: if j can recognize the desire of i to change the belief of j in way that is consistent with p, then he knows what i wants him to think. If i believes all this to happen, then it seems right to describe this belief with the words "person i means p".

This view of meaning also has a very elegant structure. It is self-referential by describing the production of a belief change and the recognized intention of the same belief change, in a way that these things point to each other. It evokes, in the reader's mind, a sense of a closed form. Meaning is described as something that occurs when things are in a self-supporting order.

So far so good, but now let us discuss the question of higher-order beliefs more precisely. Here is a re-formulation of the same definition of meaning – slightly longer and less elegant, but directly applicable to the concepts in this book. We may say that person i means p if she believes that:

(a) j will react to a^i in a way that is consistent with a belief change that is consistent with p,

(b) j believes that i believes (a), and

(c) j's belief described in (b) is the justification for j's reaction described in (a).

This definition is self-referential, too, but avoids using the word "intention" – whose proper use would require long discussions – and replaces it by describing only beliefs. Person i believes three things about person j that describe how i realizes what j realizes, thereby lending a purpose to her statement a^i.

Upon careful re-reading of the definition, we notice that the definition uses first-order beliefs and third-order beliefs. In (a), person i's first-order talking belief is that j shows some reaction to a^i. In (b) and (c), person i considers person j's second-order listening belief, about how i thinks that j shows some reaction to a^i. From i's perspective, this is a third-order belief. Without this third-order belief, the definition would not work.

But is the inclusion of this third-order belief in the definition *necessary* for describing an effective communication? The answer is no. Persons i and j can communicate effectively even if their lower-order beliefs are what they are for other reasons than having an accurate third-order belief.

First, observe that part (a) works just by itself. Person i can think that j shows a certain reaction to a^i, and it may therefore be optimal for her to choose a^i. One does not need a further justification for this first-order talking belief. It is good if the justification exists – perhaps, without it one may not want to call the concept "meaning" – but the described effect (and its measurement) are possible if one restricts attention to the outermost layer of beliefs.

Similarly, second-order beliefs work even if they are not justified by deeper beliefs. That is, we can replace (b) and (c), by saying that in addition to (a), person i believes that:

(b') j has a belief change that is consistent with p when hearing a^i, and

(c') j's belief change described in (b') is the justification for j's reaction described in (a).

The combination of i's belief in (a), (b') and (c') is simpler – it uses only first-order talking beliefs and second-order talking beliefs. It describes a perfectly fine justification for i's decision to make the statement a^i: she wants to induce the action described in (a) and she believes to achieve it by inducing the belief change described in (b').

This is the combination of beliefs that was described in Chapter 8, from the talker's perspective. In Chapter 7, an analogous combination of beliefs was given for the listener's perspective. As the two chapters demonstrate, these combinations of beliefs allow to describe many inferences from statements, and many related phenomena.

Thinking back to these chapters, we notice that there was no mention of a proposition p in them. But this makes no difference, as the chapters talked about certain updates – we can add "... that are consistent with proposition p" in our minds, without changing the content of the discussion.

Is the combination of i's belief in (a), (b') and (c') really a perfectly fine justification for the statement a^i? Perhaps not just as fine as in the earlier version, i's belief in (a), (b) and (c)?

Yes, indeed it is fine, and this is exactly the point of this book. There is a big difference between i's belief in (a), (b) and (c) on the one hand, and i's belief in (a), (b') and (c') on the other hand: the latter combination includes the possibility of false beliefs. More precisely, the second-order belief (b') may be off target, whereas the third-order belief (b), and hence also the second-order beliefs that it implies, is on target: i believes j's beliefs to be accurate.

Taken together, the discussion in this chapter means that we can use a definition of meaning that is close enough to the literature's standard, but with a lower order of beliefs and with a more general set of potentially false beliefs.

The reader should also notice that this definitory discussion of meaning is not the core of the book. It is more a feel-good observation at the end that tells us that we are done, and it is one that we do not need in order to understand the rest. Instead, the book's focus lies on the 18 questions themselves and their empirical nature, asking about the interlocutors' many ways of having possibly distorted beliefs.

Of course, none of the above discussion rules out that third-order beliefs exist in communication, and they may even be highly relevant as possible underpinnings of first-order beliefs and second-order beliefs. Whether or not they are relevant in this fashion is another open empirical question.

Chapter 10

Conclusion

Why describe communication through beliefs? The answer was given in Chapter 2: we can unambiguously describe beliefs as either accurate or inaccurate, in a measurable way. This is not a small feat.

In any real-world conversation, one cannot actually measure the answer, however. To return to the imagery in Chapter 1, we do not live through the same conversation 1000 times. But the measurement works at least in theory. If the conversation is really important, a researcher may mimick it in the laboratory, perhaps even 1000 times. Or, perhaps it helps to merely go through the thought experiment of measuring it.

The considerations in this book describe this approach. They specify the space in which the beliefs live, so that 18 questions can be asked in a well-defined way. They also give a sense of each question's scope.

The main sense that the reader should have about the scope, by now: it is large. Misunderstandings are a whole world out there. The fact that the book highlights *mis*understandings is, of course, also an expositional choice. The book's message could have been more upbeat and optimistic, by highlighting accurate understandings. This would likely create less interest, however: theories of full understanding abound in the existing literature, whereas theories of misunderstandings do not. Moreover, the data are what they are. In the majority of cases, the empirical evidence indicates the prevalence of false beliefs.

Back to detail, one last time – there is some trickery involved in the book's assumptions. Perhaps most importantly, the analysis rests on subjective expected utility, which is a bit of a black box. In addition, much of the

    https://doi.org/10.11647/OBP.0367.10

uncertainty is about a very general "state" ω. Many other approaches, with more or less structure, would have been possible as alternatives for Chapter 2. For instance, the book could have combined the state of the world and an interlocutor's type into a single item. (In game theory, they are often subsumed under a single category "type".) Note also how the use of a time structure is somewhat special in the book – it is not quite modelled in the formulae (except for the distinction between a^j and $\tilde{a}^j$ in Chapters 5 and 8) but a sequential interaction is implicit in the discussion.

All of these modelling choices in the book are fairly arbitrary – or rather, they are made mainly for clarity in the argumentation rather than for realism. For instance, the separation of a discussion of preference types allows to address all questions of interest alingment head-on. The exposition also serves to connect the book to existing literatures (see the section "Further reading" in Chapter 11). Overall, the maintained assumptions may or may not be more realistic than other assumptions that one could make. But as assumptions go, at least they are quite weak.

Finally, recall that the direction that is expressed in the questions' formulation is idiosyncratic. Beliefs can be off target in many ways; the book only formulates the possibility of too little discriminaton. Why not overoptimism, motivated belief biases, or probability weighting? There are so many more patterns in which humans may systematically screw up their probabilistic thinking, and the book uses only one of them. Let us, thus, view the book's brevity as a statement about the many routes that research on biases in communication can take.

Chapter 11

Bibliography and further reading

Bibliographic references

Agranov, Marina, Utteeyo Dasgupta and Andrew Schotter (2023), Trust Me: Communication and Competition in Psychological Games, *Working Paper*, Division of the Humanities and Social Sciences, California Institute of Technology.

Barner, David, and Jesse Snedeker (2008), Compositionality and Statistics in Adjective Acquisition: 4-Year-Olds Interpret Tall and Short Based on the Size Distributions of Novel Noun Referents, *Child Development* 79(3), 594-608.

Belot, Michèle, V. Bhaskar and Jeroen van de Ven (2012), Can observers predict trustworthiness?, *The Review of Economics and Statistics* 94(1), 246-259.

Binzel, Christine, and Dietmar Fehr (2013), Social distance and trust: Experimental evidence from a slum in Cairo, *Journal of Development Economics* 103, 99-106.

Camerer, Colin, George Loewenstein, and Martin Weber (1998), The Curse of Knowledge in Economic Settings: An Experimental Analysis, *The Journal of Political Economy* 97(5), 1232-1254.

Carlson, Erika N., and R. Michael Furr (2009), Evidence of Differential

https://doi.org/10.11647/OBP.0367.11

Meta-Accuracy, *Psychological Science* 20(8), 1033-1039.

Charness, Gary, and Martin Dufwenberg (2006), Promises and Partnerships, *Econometrica* 74(6), 1579-1601.

Dufwenberg, Martin, Simon Gächter and Heike Hennig-Schmidt (2011), The framing of games and the psychology of play, *Games and Economic Behavior* 73, 459-478.

Eyster, Erik, Matthew Rabin and Georg Weizsäcker (2018), An Experiment on Social Mislearning, *CRC TRR 190 Discussion Paper 73.*

Gilovich, Thomas, Kenneth Savitsky and Victoria Husted Medvec (1998), The Illusion of Transparency: Biased Assessments of Others' Ability to Read One's Emotional States, *Journal of Personality and Social Psychology* 72(2), 332-346.

Gordon, Anne K., and Arthur G. Miller (2000), Perspective Differences in the Construal of Lies: Is Deception in the Eye of the Beholder?, *Personality and Social Psychology Bulletin* 26(1), 46-55.

Grabova, Iuliia, Hedda Nielsen and Georg Weizsäcker (2023), *Attempting to detect a lie: Do we think it through?*, Working Paper, Humboldt-Universität zu Berlin.

Griffin, Dale, and Amos Tversky (1992), The Weighing of Evidence and the Determinants of Confidence, *Cognitive Psychology* 24, 411-434.

Holtgraves, Thomas, and Joong-Nam Yang (1990), Politeness as Universal: Cross-Cultural Perceptions of Request Strategies and Inferences Based on Their Use, *Journal of Personality and Social Psychology* 59(4), 719-729.

Peltzer, Isabel (2019), *Do we ignore that they judge us in context? The Effect of Context on Beliefs.* Master thesis, Humboldt Universität zu Berlin.

Ross, Lee D., Teresa M. Amabile and Julia L. Steinmetz (1977), Social Roles, Social Control, and Biases in Social-Perception Processes, *Journal of Personality and Social Psychology* 35(7), 485-494.

Savitzky, Kenneth, Boaz Keysar, Nicholas Epley, Travis Carter and Ashley Swanson (2011), The closeness-communication bias: Increased egocentrism among friends versus strangers, *Journal of Experimental Social Psychology* 47, 269-273.

Sheremeta, Roman M., and Timothy W. Shields (2013), Do liars believe? Beliefs and other-regarding preferences in sender–receiver games, *Journal of Economic Behavior and Organization* 94, 268-277.

Further reading

As complement for **Chapter 1**, and perhaps the entire book, the following seven works give surveys of the many applications of communication in different disciplines. The list is selective but the reader finds many more references in these texts. The list also supports the claims about the literature in Chapter 1.

A useful survey of communication experiments in economics:

- Blume, Andreas, Ernest K. Lai and Wooyoung Kim (2020), Strategic Information Transmission: A Survey of Experiments and Theoretical Foundations, in C.M. Capra, Rachel T.A. Croson, Mary L. Rigdon and Tanya S. Rosenblat (eds.), *Handbook of Experimental Game Theory*, Elgar.

The following is a fun-to-read-but-precise overview of psychological evidence of how little we understand the minds of others. The book includes many references to findings that are specific to communication, including misunderstandings.

- Epley, Nicholas (2015), *Mindwise.* Penguin Books.

An earlier account of misunderstandings, from a sociological perspective, is in the following volume.

- Young, Robert L. (1999), *Understanding misunderstandings: A practical guide to more successful human interaction.* University of Texas Press.

For theory-minded economists, the following handbook chapter has a good introduction to both the theory and the wide set of applications of strategic communication in economics and organizations. It shows the strong focus that economists put on equilibrium thinking.

- Gibbons, Robert, Niko Matouschek and John Roberts (2013), *Decisions in Organizations*, in: Gibbons, Robert, Niko Matouschek and John Roberts (editors), *The Handbook of Organizational Economics*, Princeton University Press.

Among the set of social sciences, political science is special in that communication has long been established as a really big topic. Actually, as a whole subdiscipline, as described in this large handbook.

- Kaid, Lynda Lee (editor) (2004), *Handbook of Political Communication Research*. Lawrence Erlbaum Associates.

An insightful and recent economics book collects evidence on an important part of communication: advice. The book highlights how advice and societal conventions are intertwined.

- Schotter, Andrew (2023), *Advice, Social Learning, and the Evolution of Conventions*. Cambridge University Press.

A concise and fairly recent overview of linguistic studies on misunderstandings appears in the following article.

- Padilla Cruz, Manuel (2017), Interlocutors-Related and Hearer-Specific Causes of Misunderstanding: Processing Strategy, Confirmation Bias and Weak Vigilance, *Research in Language (RiL)* 1, 11-36.

The formal set-up of the analysis in **Chapter 2** is close to the typical ones in game theory. The following two textbooks are classics in this field. The first is more technical and has a deeper coverage of information structures in games of incomplete information. The second focusses more on applications from economics and political science. A nice connection of this book to the present one is that many of its analyses are described for general, non-equilibrium beliefs.

- Fudenberg, Drew, and Jean Tirole (1991). *Game Theory*. MIT Press.

- Osborne, Martin (2002). *An Introduction to Game Theory*. Oxford University Press.

The following book made an important conceptual contribution to both pragmatics and game theory, by describing the concept of common knowledge for the first time. (In economics, Robert Aumann introduced it several years later but pretty much independently.) The book is a game-theoretic treatise of language, and everything is in equilibrium here.

- Lewis, David (1969), *Convention: A Philosophical Study.* Harvard University Press.

A broad decision-theoretic textbook with an introduction to subjective expected utility and its many variants is found here:

- Wakker, Peter P. (2010), *Prospect Theory: For Risk and Ambiguity.* Cambridge University Press.

The distinction between discrimination and calibration, mentioned first in **Chapter 3**, is attributed to Allan H. Murphy and has its roots in the literature on forecasting – yet another scientific discipline that has connections to the literature on belief elicitation. The following list of articles includes also other works that give an overview of belief elicitation.

- Armantier, Olivier, and Nicolas Treich (2013), Eliciting beliefs: Proper scoring rules, incentives, stakes and hedging. *European Economic Review* 62, 17-40.

- Hollard, Guillaume, Sebastien Massoni and Jean-Christophe Vergnaud (2016), In search of good probability assessors: an experimental comparison of elicitation rules for confidence judgments. *Theory and Decision* 80, 363-387.

- Murphy, Allan H. (1998), The Early History of Probability Forecasts: Some Extensions and Clarifications. *Weather and Forecasting* 13, 5-15. The paper describes the history of forecasting literature, including references to Murphy's own work.

- Schotter, Andrew, and Isabel Trevino (2014). Belief Elicitation in the Laboratory. *Annual Review of Economics* 6, 103–128.

A useful overview of the many applications of belief data in economics is given by the following volume:

- Bachmann, Rüdiger, Giorgio Topa, and Wilbert van der Klaauw (editors) (2022), *Handbook of Economic Expectations*, Elsevier.

The reader may have noticed that Chapter 3 does not present evidence that is specific to communication. The failure to connect with communication research owes to the generally rather juvenile state of the literature that covers experiments on communication beliefs.

Yet, the chapter introduces many of the book's main concepts. The distinction between manifest and known is a key element of relevance theory, a theory with big impact on the entire field of pragmatics, including many ideas that appear in this book. The following is the main bibliographic reference for this theory. (Note: this references the book's second edition, of 1995. The first edition appeared in 1986.)

- Sperber, Dan, and Deirdre Wilson (1995), *Relevance: Communication & Cognition. Second Edition.* Blackwell Publishsing.

Another important concept of Chapter 3 is context dependence of conversations. Context dependence, too, is a defining element of the field of pragmatics. Where its importance was first recognized is unknown (to the author) but a frequent reference in the current literature is a collection of philosophical papers by Herbert H. Clark and his co-authors.

- Clark, Herbert H. (1992), *Arenas of Language Use.* University of Chicago Press and Center for the Study of Language and Information.

Chapter 3's two other main concepts are belief biases (mainly discussed in Question 2) and the possible neglect of type-specific actions (Question 1). Each of them follows a wide literature and on both of them, a recent handbook provides a good literature survey:

- Benjamin, Daniel (2019), Errors in probabilistic reasoning and judgment biases. Chapter 2 in: Bernheim, B. Douglas, Stefano Della Vigna, and David Laibson (editors), *Handbook of Behavioral Economics – Foundations and Applications 2.* North-Holland.

- Eyster, Erik (2019), Errors in Strategic Reasoning. Chapter 3 in: Bernheim, B. Douglas, Stefano Della Vigna, and David Laibson (editors), *Handbook of Behavioral Economics – Foundations and Applications 2.* North-Holland.

On the possible neglect of type-specific actions: this behavioral bias has become highly influential in behavioral economics, due to the following contribution, among others:

- Eyster, Erik, and Matthew Rabin (2005), Cursed Equilibrium, *Econometrica* 73(5), 1632-1673.

Yet, the bias has only very recently been expressed in the form of theoretical models that are tailored to sequential games, like commmunication games. Two relevant studies – with nicely fitting titles – are:

- Cohen, Shani, and Shengwu Li (2023), *Sequential Cursed Equilibrium*, Working Paper, Harvard University.

- Fong, Meng-Jhang, Po-Hsuan Lin, and Thomas R. Palfrey (2023), *Cursed Sequential Equilibrium*, Working Paper, California Institute of Technology.

As a final comment on Chapter 3, the psychological evidence on correspondence bias is covered extensively in Epley (2015), cited above. A classic publication on this effect is the following article.

- Gilbert, Daniel T., and Patrick S. Malone (1995), The Correspondence Bias. *Psychological Bulletin* 117, 21-38.

Chapter 4's initial statements about language as a convention refers mainly to Lewis's (1969) contribution that is cited above. The term "talking beliefs", and their precise description, does not appear in the previous literature, to the author's knowledge. However, many of the `empirical papers` cited throughout the book report belief data that have precisely this format.

The question of more or less informative equilibria, including the possibility of babbling equilibria, is a classic and wide discussion in the game theory of strategic transmission. In addition to the overview paper of Gibbons et al. (2013), cited above, the following two articles are noteworthy. The first is a substantial article that started a whole literature, discussing formally the possible equilibria in "cheap talk" communication games where the talker has an objective function that is different from that of the listener. The second is an elegant survey of what communication is possible and impossible, in theory.

- Crawford, Vincent P., and Joel Sobel (1982), Strategic Information Transmission. *Econometrica* 50, 1431-1451.

- Sobel, Joel (2020), Lying and Deception in Games, *Journal of Political Economy* 128(3), 907-947.

The chapter also includes a brief discussion of the use of monetary incentives in experiments (continued in the subsequent chapter). This is actually a fundamental methodological discussion that is as old as the entire research field. The reader can obtain an in-depth treatment of this discussion, and of many other methodological issues, in the following textbook.

- Bardsley, Nicholas, Robin Cubitt, Graham Loomes, Peter Moffatt, Chris Starmer, and Robert Sugden (2020), *Experimental Economics – Rethinking the Rules*. Princeton University Press.

The reference to the "art of questioning" and affective questions points to the largely empirical and interdisciplinary field of communication studies. Insights from this field also enter in Chapter 5, in the discussion of the personal characteristics of the talker. They are contained in the following overview book.

- Hargie, Owen (2017), *Skilled Interpersonal Communication: Research, Theory and Practice. Sixth Edition*. Routledge.

Chapter 4 connects the discussion of the listener's type with that of (im)politeness. Politeness is an established subliterature within linguistics, as the following works show. The first is a well-written and very accessible linguistic textbook that summarizes many key concepts used in this book. The second is a collection of mostly empirical studies on the liguistics of impoliteness. Throughout the book, snippets of recorded conversations illustrate quite impressively how fast and efficient human interlocutors can be when it comes to producing impolite utterances. The book also shows a major difference between experimental psychology/economics and (large parts of) the empirical research in linguistics: the latter uses naturally occurring data far more frequently than the former.

- Birner, Betty J. (2013), *Introduction to Pragmatics*. Wiley-Blackwell.

- Bousfield, Derek, and Miriam A. Locher (eds.) (2008), *Impoliteness in Language: Studies on its Interplay with Power in Theory and Practice*. Mouton de Gruyter.

The classic piece of work on speech acts is the following by John L. Austin. He is one of the grandfathers in the field of philsoophy of language – and he only needs the book's title to show his skill. A modern treatment of the lectures that his book contains, and subsequent material, appears in Birner (2013), cited above.

- Austin, John L. (1962), *How to do things with words*. Oxford University Press.

A very good discussion of how the importance of context speaks against the view of language as a convention can be found in the introductory chapter of Sperber and Wilson (1995), cited above.

Chapter 4 also introduces the most important thought of the present book that is translated from Sperber and Wilson's (1995) book: the idea that the talker identifies relevance and (in Chapter 7) that the listener expects the same from the talker. Upon inspection of the translation, one may notice that the present book defines the (perceived) relevance of a context, whereas Sperber and Wilson discuss the relevance of a statement. In each case, the important emphasis of the discussion lies on the interaction between a statement and its context. Both variants of "relevance" serve this purpose and describe, by and large, the same psychological phenomenon.

Chapter 5 describes the possible significance of the fact that the talker talks at all (instead of being silent). This is another important part of Sperber and Wilson's (1995) relevance theory: the tacit guarantee of relevance. (Empirically speaking, the listener may miss it.) Chapter 7 picks the same reasoning up again.

Context-dependent listening (Question 9) is described as a simple step in the direction of meaning. This relates *inter alia* to the works of Clark (1992) and Sperber and Wilson (1995) that were cited above. The earlier and even more classic references to such context-dependent meaning are the works by H. Paul Grice that he wrote, roughly, during the forty-year span after 1945 and that are collected in this book:

- Grice, H.P. (1989), *Studies in the Way of Words*, Harvard University Press.

The theoretical properties of incentive mechanisms that pay money for reported beliefs, also discussed in Chapter 5, are well-understood by now. Recent noteworthy contributions include the following two. The first collects a wide set of theoretical knowledge, and empirical assessments, about scoring rules. The second contains the mechanism described in the text.

- Schlag, Karl H., James Tremewan, and Joel van der Weele (2015), A penny for your thoughts: a survey of methods for eliciting beliefs. *Experimental Economics* 18, 457-490.

- Hossain, Tanjim, and Ryo Okui (2013), The Binarized Scoring Rule. *Review of Economic Studies* 80, 984-1001.

The behavioral reaction of experimental participants to incentive rules – including the observation that the data quality depends on the payment, has been examined in numerous experiments. Recent ones are by Hollard et al. (2016), cited above, and the following three.

- Trautmann, Stefan, and Gijs van de Kuilen (2015), Belief elicitation: A horse race among truth serums. *The Economic Journal* 125, 2116–2135.

- Charness, Gary, Uri Gneezy, and Vlastimil Rasocha (2021), Experimental methods: Eliciting beliefs. *Journal of Economic Behavior and Organzation* 189, 234-256.

- Danz, David, Lise Vesterlund, and Alistair Wilson (2022), Belief Elicitation and Behavioral Incentive Compatibility. *American Economic Review* 112(9), 2851–2883.

The discussion in **Chapter 6** relies on large literatures in psychology and behavioral economics, on misperceived mental models of other people. The two bodies of literature in these two fields are quite different in nature, and the above-cited works by Epley (2015) and Eyster (2019) give comprehensive introductions. Another very useful introduction to the economic models of misperceived opponents, which also has a section on communication games, is here:

- Crawford, Vincent P., Miguel A. Costa-Gomes, and Nagore Irriberri (2013), Structural Models of Nonequilibrium Strategic Thinking: Theory, Evidence, and Applications. *Journal of Economic Literature* 51, 5-62.

An important part of this literature is the general idea that economic agents take into account that other economic agents make errors. If this taking-into-account follows rational-expectations assumptions and there is common knowledge about this fact, the model prediction is that of Quantal Response Equilibrium. The seminal article on it is

- McKelvey, Richard D., and Thomas R. Palfrey (1995), Quantal Response Equilibria for Normal Form Games. *Games and Economic Behavior* 10, 6-38.

Two well-known articles about psychological games, another item of discussion in Chapter 6, are the following:

- Geanakoplos, John, David Pearce, and Ennio Stacchetti (1989), Psychological Games and Sequential Rationality. *Games and Economic Behavior* 1, 60-79.

- Rabin, Matthew (1993), Incorporating Fairness into Game Thery and Economics. *American Economic Review* 83, 1281-1302.

The methodology on collecting second-order beliefs is far less widely researched than that for first-order beliefs. The following article is sometimes cited as the seminal one.

- Manski, Charles F., and Claudia Neri (2013), First- and second-order subjective expectations in strategic decision-making: Experimental evidence. *Games and Economic Behavior* 81, 232-254.

Chapter 7 contains the first portion of the book's main discussion about pragmatic meaning. The argumentation is oriented at relevance theory as described in Sperber and Wilson (1995), cited above.

The following book contains another closely related analysis of language. It describes how context-dependent signals and beliefs can carry meaning with few steps of reasoning. Like the present book, it follows an empirical approach to language. Its main focus lies on the origin of language, arguing that much knowledge about human communication can be learned from measuring communication of animals.

- Tomasello, Michael (2008), *Origins of Human Communication.* MIT Press.

A wide overview of many empirical findings of lie detection (often, the lack thereof) is in the following book:

- Vrij, Aldert (2008), *Detecting Lies and Deceipt: Pitfalls and Opportunities.* John Wiley & Sons.

Another classic reference for the difficulty of lie detection is the following article:

- Bond, Charles F. Jr., and Bella M. DePaulo (2006), Accuracy of Deception Judgements, *Personality and Social Psychology Review* 10(3), 214-234.

A comunication game that allows measuring the frequency of lying – a different game that is not covered in this book but has received wide attention – is examined in the following two papers. The first is the original reference to the game, the second is a meta-study:

- Fischbacher, Urs, and Franziska Föllmi-Heusi (2013), Lies in Disguise—An Experimental Study on Cheating. *Journal of the European Economic Association* 11(3), 525-547.

- Abeler, Johannes, Daniele Nosenzo, and Collin Raymond (2019), Preferences for Truth-Telling. *Econometrica* 87(4), 1115-1153.

A study of white lies in an experimental game can be found here:

- Gneezy, Uri (2005), Deception: The Role of Consequences. *American Economic Review* 95(1), 384-394.

The "mirrorred" game, which Grabova et al. (2023) use to observe a full set of talking beliefs and listening beliefs, was introduced in the following article:

- Peeters, Ronald, Marc Vorsatz, and Marcus Walzl (2015), Beliefs and truth-telling: A laboratory experiment. *Journal of Economic Behavior and Organization* 113, 1-12.

The main discussions in **Chapter 8** also use insights from the game-theoretic and relevance-theoretic works, contained e.g. in Sobel (2020) and Sperber and Wilson (1995), both cited above. The discussion of linguistic vagueness draws on insights summarized in the following overview chapter:

- van Rooij, Robert (2011), Vagueness and linguistics. In: Ronzitti, Gabriella (ed.), *Vagueness: A Guide*. Springer.

Chapter 9's main part refers to Grice's notion of speaker's meaning. The definition with beliefs in (a), (b) and (c) is adapted from the exposition in Sperber and Wilson (1995), cited above. For very useful discussion of intentions in communication, the reader is referred to Tomassello (2008), also cited above.

Index

action, 10-108, 114

affective question, 38, 116

art of questioning, 37, 116

Aumann, Robert, 112

Austin, John L., 116

babbling equilibrium, 35-36, 79, 115

belief, 2-108, 112-120

belief elicitation, 18, 20-21, 25, 34-35, 38-40, 49-51, 63-64, 67, 77-78, 113, 119

belief measurement, *see* belief elicitation

calibration, 18, 22-23, 113

cheap talk, 115

circumstance, 12, 23, 32-35, 47-48, 66, 69, 74-76, 78, 80-81, 83, 89, 91-92

Clark, Herbert H., 114

common ground, 26

common knowledge, 15, 112, 118

context, 4-6, 26-29, 42-45, 55-56, 65-71, 84-87, 96-100, 114, 117, 119 convention, 31-32, 35, 42, 84, 102, 112, 115, 117

co-presence, 66-67, 70

correspondence bias, 28, 115

deception, *see* lie

decision theory, 14, 113

dictator game, 44

discrimination, 18, 22-23, 27, 37, 51, 58, 63-64, 68, 101, 108, 113

Draghi, Mario, 4-5

equilibrium, 35-36, 79, 93, 111-112, 114-115

expectation, *see* belief

experiment, 20-28, 34-36, 39-41, 44-45, 50-51, 54-59, 63, 68-71, 77-99, 111-120

experimenter demand, 54

external validity, 67

first-order belief, *see* belief

first-order talking belief, *see* talking belief

first-order listening belief, *see* listening belief

framing manipulation, 70-71

game theory, 5-6, 14, 35-36, 69, 79, 108, 112, 115

Grice, H. Paul, 117, 120

Griffin, Dale, 25

guilt aversion, 69, 99

higher-order beliefs (third-order or higher), 6, 94, 97, 101-105

hindsight bias, 68

illusion of transparency, 63, 91-92

indirect inference, 39

information, 7, 11, 13-100, 112

information structure, 11, 15, 24, 44, 80, 112

intention, 5, 102-103, 120

interlocutor, 13-15, 39, 44, 53, 66-68, 76, 82, 97, 102, 105, 108, 116

issue, 10-12, 15-16, 24, 27, 31

Laschet, Armin, 5

lie, 76, 79-84, 99, 102, 120

lie detection, 81-82, 119

listening belief, 48-59, 62, 65, 73-87, 89-103, 120

lying aversion, 36-37, 99-100

manifest, 11, 23, 27, 48, 55, 62, 65-67, 96, 114

meaning, 74-75, 84, 90, 96-97, 102-105, 117, 119-120

measurement of beliefs, *see* belief elicitation

mentalize, *see* second-order belief

meta-accuracy 52, 64

misunderstanding, 2-3, 5-7, 44, 66, 70, 81-83, 95, 101, 107, 111-112

monetary incentives / monetary payments, 56-58, 115

Murphy, Allan H., 113

negative face, 38

open question, 38-39

ostension, 94, 97

perceived relevance, 42-43, 53, 56, 66, 74, 84-85, 97, 117

perspective taking, 82-83

politeness, 38, 40-41, 69, 102, 116

pragmatics, 3-4, 112, 114, 116

preference, 6, 11-12, 35, 37, 57-58, 81-83, 94, 108

power, 69-70

psychological game theory, 69, 118

public-good game, 70

random role assignment, 28

relevance theory, 114, 117, 119

revealed expectation, 40

salesman pitch, 36

second-order belief, 6-7, 61-105, 119

second-order listening belief, 74-87, 91, 95, 97, 103

second-order talking belief, 90-101, 104

speech act, 41-42, 116

Sperber, Dan, 117

state / state of the world, 10-108

subjective expected utility, 7, 14-15, 57, 76, 107, 113

talking belief, 33-45, 49, 62, 65, 74, 77-87, 89-104, 115, 120

trust game, 21, 51

Tversky, Amos, 25

type, 10-99, 108, 114, 116

utility, 2, 7, 13-16, 18, 22-23, 26-27, 32, 37-38, 41-43, 47-50, 56-57, 66, 69, 76, 80-81, 84, 90, 97, 107, 113

vagueness, 92-95, 120

Wilson, Deirdre, 117

white lie, 79-82, 120

Author's acknowledgements

A first shout-out goes to my students. Over the summer terms of six years, the Master's-level students in the course "Behavioral Economics" at Humboldt-Universität zu Berlin discussed the contents of this book with me. In each cohort, the students created a scholarly atmosphere with insightful discussions and they gave me, along the way, much help to improve the book.

Another relevant group is our Berlin-Munich research center, funded by the German Research Foundation: the Collaborative Research Center Transregio 190 "Rationality and Competition". I started working on the book around the time when the center's activities started, and through them I received the intellectual stimuli and personal encouragements that I needed for the book's completion. Thank you to my fantastic colleagues.

And similarly to all other colleagues at Humboldt – students, faculty, administrators alike – thank you for such a good time in the office. Special times, also very good ones, were had during two extended research stays at Stanford and NYU. Without these visits, the book may never have grown.

Numerous colleagues, friends and family members gave me specific feedback on the manuscript or made conversational comments that were helpful for writing the book. I surely forget many of these instances but do not want to leave out the names of people whom I remember in this context: Kai Barron, Jonathan Beck, Gary Charness, Timm Dusemund, Florian Englmaier, Nicholas Epley, Erik Eyster, Nicola Garbarino, Hanna Ginsborg, Iuliia Grabova, Peter Haan, Gerhard Haase-Hindenberg, Jan-Ottmar Hesse, Steffen Huck, Andreas Isenschmid, Camilla Karnau, Dorothea Kübler, So Jung Lee, Kathleen Ngangoué, Hedda Nielsen, Ronald Peeters, Tobias Rosefeldt, Alvin Roth, Ariel Rubinstein, Klaus Schmidt, Andrew Schotter, Sebastian Schweighofer-Kodritsch, Joel Sobel, Bruno Veltri, Emanuel Vespa, Fintan Viebahn, Daniel Warren, Lorenz Weizsäcker, Mirko Wiederholt and Alistair Wilson.

The publishing house deserves its own praise. The book is an open-access publication, which is possible only because of the tireless and professional work of Rupert Gatti and Alessandra Tosi, together with all their colleagues at OBP. They do a great service to the scientific community.

Finally, I thank my closest family: Dorothea, our two children, my parents and siblings. Writing a book takes a long time and requires a deep support system, which I am lucky to have in you.

In my saying "thank you", I want to single out Dorothea for so much love and reason.

www.ingramcontent.com/pod-product-compliance
Lightning Source LLC
Chambersburg PA
CBHW050044220326
41599CB00045B/7278